Compassionate Woman

Compassionate Woman

the Life *and* Legacy *of* Patricia Locke

JOHN KOLSTOE

Bahá'í
PUBLISHING
Wilmette, Illinois

Bahá'í Publishing
415 Linden Avenue, Wilmette, Illinois 60091-2844
Copyright © 2011 by the National Spiritual Assembly of the Bahá'ís of the
United States

All rights reserved. Published 2011
Printed in the United States of America on acid-free paper ∞

14   13   12   11   4   3   2   1

Library of Congress Cataloging-in-Publication Data

Kolstoe, John E.

  Compassionate Woman : the life and legacy of Patricia Locke / by John
Kolstoe.

     p. cm.

  Includes bibliographical references.

  ISBN 978-1-931847-85-8 (acid-free paper) 1. Locke, Patricia, 1928–2001.
2. Locke, Patricia, 1928–2001—Influence. 3. Teton Indians—Biography. 4.
Indian women—United States—Biography. 5. Women social reformers—United
States—Biography. 6. Women political activists—United States--Biography.
7. Bahai women—United States—Biography. 8. Indians of North America—
Education—West (U.S.)—History—20th century. 9. Social justice—West
(U.S.)—History—20th century. 10. National Women's Hall of Fame (Seneca
Falls, N.Y.)—Biography. I. Title.

  E99.T34L635 2011

  303.48'4092—dc22

  [B]

                                                                    2011002946

Cover design by Andrew Johnson
Book design by Patrick Falso
Photograph on cover by Don Doll

Patricia Locke (1928–2001) wrote her own, most fitting, dedication. Shortly before she died she asked for some paper and a pen. For more than an hour she labored over her writing, and finally she lay back in the bed exhausted. But she finished her work—the final statement from her exquisite pen. In small handwriting were these words, which serve as the dedication to this book:

To the Bahá'í Youth of the world: We come to you in loving consultation.

The Locke family

Contents

Author's Notes
and Acknowledgments

A large portrait of Patricia Locke in Kevin Locke's home caught my attention. I asked who was writing his mother's biography. Kevin said, "Well, no one." Patricia's granddaughter Maymangwa Flying Earth-Miranda wanted to, but circumstances stopped her. Somewhat surprised, I said it needed to be done and I had some ideas about people who might do it. So, I approached some folks.

The first one approached was Pauline Tuttle, a Micmac Indian from Canada, who had done her PhD thesis in ethnomusicology. She agreed to take on the challenge. Unfortunately, cancer claimed her life before the work really started. A few other people were approached without success. Still, the biography needed to be written. So, it was left to me.

Anyone who knew Pat and is reading this will think of many important achievements and anecdotes that could have been included. They are right. There is no attempt to provide a complete list of either her activities or accomplishments. Instead vignettes have been selected to give a verbal portrait of this remarkable woman. As her friend Frances Makepeace pointed out, Pat was a beautiful tapestry that you can't take apart. She was complex and all her many activities were interwoven. This book is a glimpse of that tapestry.

During interviews conducted to learn more about Pat, I was struck by how many people said that it was after her passing that they realized how many other things she had done. Her skill, competence, and commitment to whatever she was doing was such that many people who worked with her assumed that the project they were working on together was as all consuming for her as it was for them. They were surprised, if not astounded, to learn that it was but one of the many "all consuming" projects she was doing simultaneously.

There will be a happy day when Maymangwa can finally write of her grandmother. That will be a much different book than this in terms of intimacy, perspective, and information, but well worth reading.

Pat liked to be known by her Lakota Name, Tȟawáčhiŋ Wašté Wíŋ (Compassionate Woman), which she received as an adult. In addition to the honor of the name, it illustrates her passion for the preservation of Indian cultures and languages. For this reason, Lakota orthography is shown throughout the book and in a glossary of terms relevant to her story.

Pat left a rich legacy of her life through recorded talks, writings, and videos. They reveal much of her view of the world. These were the windows into her thinking and interests that became the foundation of this biography.

The cooperation of Pat's family was essential for this work. Winona, Pat's daughter, made many of Pat's papers available. Kevin Locke, Pat's son, not only supplied endless information about his mother, but also gave needed background details about Lakota traditions, values, and worldview—he was the principal source of encouragement and information throughout the long process. Larry Atkinson, owner of the *Mobridge Tribune,* allowed unlimited access to the newspaper's archives because of his high regard for Pat.

Finally, a large measure of thanks must go to my wife, Janet, for having endured long hours of my preoccupation with this engaging work. The Livingston, Montana writer's group gave many valuable suggestions, and special thanks must also go to the many people who reviewed and made comments on various parts of the manuscript.

May you enjoy reading this as much as I have cherished researching and writing about this phenomenal person. Extra bounties have included the privilege of working closely with Kevin, learning so much about Lakota life, participating in sweat lodges, and attending powwows and a sun dance. What started as an offer to assist in a worthy project, turned into a love-journey of discoveries and insights.

Introduction

A blistering sun hung in the sky over the Standing Rock Reservation and shadows of clouds drifted over the prairie. Yellow butterflies fluttered in the grass, meadowlarks in the sky. Pat, who we called *Unchi* (Uŋčí, meaning *grandmother*), pointed to a distant butte where medicine men would take young men for days of fasting and praying to receive a vision from the Creator. The air was light and clear over the long green hills, over the Grand River, where Sitting Bull and the Hunkpapa once camped; clear all the way out to Bear Butte, a favored place of Crazy Horse.

"As generations come and go, some change is natural," said Unchi. "Evolution is a part of life. But we must resist the sudden intrusive changes that are imposed upon us. As indigenous people, we have to articulate what we mean by change, define what we perceive as essential to our way of life. We can't blindly accept what others call progress. Our people were warriors. And we must be warriors again. We must fight these changes forced on our way of life."

Unchi grew quiet. A meadowlark hopped toward us and a hawk swooped by in a long graceful arc, alighted for a moment on a rock, and then lifted lightly into the air, gliding away over the rim of a hill. "You know, we're not just fighting for the Lakota," said Unchi, turning toward me. "We have to fight for everyone now, and for all creatures."

Pat Locke was as warm and loving as anyone I've ever known. She was also a fierce, unyielding warrior, descended from a long line of men and women who gave their lives for their people. The great chiefs and visionaries of the past were not just legends to her, but a real presence in her life, and from them she drew courage and vision.

Near the end of his life, with many battles behind him and the burden of dark times upon his people, Sitting Bull said, "Let's get our minds together and do something good for the children." As if this great spirit was at her side or working through her, this became the heart of Unchi's lifework. This impulse to help young people sprang naturally from her great love for her own children and grand-children; and it flowed out like ripples on a pond to reach young people she would never meet. In this biography, you'll *see* how she became the moving force for founding community colleges that give young Native Americans the skills and confidence they need to make their way in this rapidly changing world.

Difficult times have a way of producing great leaders, and Un-chi battled on many difficult and challenging fronts. In addition to founding colleges for Native Americans, she fought for religious free-dom and the sacred sites of Native Americans. She became a leader of the Bahá'í Faith. She fought for tribal land rights and for a healthy environment for every person and every creature. Close to home, she worked tirelessly to foster respect between Indians and non-Indians. At international forums, she spoke out for Indigenous rights and for the rights of women.

There were many facets to Unchi's life—some public, others very private. Some who knew her well may read this book and say "Yes, but she was more than this." And they are right for her spirit was too vast, too sweet and fierce and timeless to be confined in passages and pages of a book. Yet, John Kolstoe's carefully researched and crafted biogra-phy gives us a much-needed introduction to this remarkable woman.

Over the course of her life, Unchi received many honors, includ-ing the prestigious McArthur Fellowship and being cited as the most effective Native American leader of the twentieth century. Yet, to the end she remained grounded in who she was as a Lakota woman. She loved nothing more than to be with her family. I remember a summer evening when she and her extended family walked down to the shore of the Missouri River. Her daughter Nona came with her children, and we gathered driftwood logs. We dragged them to the sweat lodge that her son Kevin made of canvas stretched over a bent willow frame. We lit a fire and laid some good-sized rocks in the heart of the flames. After the rocks had baked for about an hour, we carried them into the sweatlodge, where their heat would help purify us.

"Mitákuye Oyás'iŋ (we are all related)" Unchi said as we entered. Inside, it was completely dark. Time disappeared. We prayed and sang.

Art Davidson

I

The Funeral

They came from every direction.* There were Native Americans, Latinos, Asians, Blacks, and Whites. Some people pooled their meager
resources to drive over 1,000 miles and slept in their cars to save expenses. Others flew into Phoenix and stayed at comfortable hotels.
There were the highly educated and illiterate; people of wealth and
many who knew poverty well; some had penetrating insight and broad
vision, there were others of limited capacity; some viewed life with a
radiant spirit while others saw the world darkly; there were laborers
(skilled and unskilled), doctors, artists, students, lawyers, hairdressers,
artisans, carpenters, entrepreneurs, educators, masons, business execu-
tives, secretaries, judges, craftsmen, and the chronically unemployed.
All came to pay homage to Patricia Ann McGillis Locke, known to
many as Tȟawáčhiŋ Wašté Wíŋ (Compassionate Woman), who had
touched the lives of everyone there in so many different ways.

---

* To the traditional Lakota, directions are more than points on a map or com-
pass. They speak of the four sacred directions, each associated with a sacred color
as well as with songs. Each color has many symbolic meanings, including specific
characteristics of the Great Spirit, as well as representing all the races and ethnic
groups of humanity and everything that lives in those regions—the two-legged and
four-legged, the winged ones, the finned ones, and the crawling ones, as well as the
earth itself. Reference to the four directions suggests the interconnectedness and
sacredness of all creation.

A drum being played during her funeral.

It was her funeral, but the diversity of those who came was an eloquent testament of her life. The proceedings were broadcast live over KLND, the radio station of her home on the Standing Rock Reservation, which she helped found, and for which she had labored as a boardmember for so many years. People who could not attend, listened for three hours to the many relatives and friends who came forward to pay their respects and give tributes to Tȟawáčhiŋ Wašté Wíŋ.

Robert Henderson, a colleague of hers on the National Spiritual Assembly of the Bahá'ís of the United States,* summed up the thoughts of many when he said, "We must not let our sense of loss prevent us from celebrating a life that was so beautifully lived and realized. Pat Locke was a flower in full bloom at the peak of power and the fragrance of her life will linger in our hearts throughout our lives. Her spiritual qualities, her nobility of character will be an inspiration to all of us, every day of our lives."[1]

Who was this Lakota woman of humble origin for whom obstacles were the ladder of life? Against all odds she got a college education. She was a leader and spokesperson on behalf of the down-

---

* See Chapter XIV for the function and importance of the National Spiritual Assembly within the Bahá'í administrative framework.

trodden of all ethnic groups. She was instrumental in establishing seventeen colleges on Indian Reservations, and helped empower tribes to establish their own school curricula. She fought for Native language preservation, the environment, the rights of women, Native rights, self-determination, and heritage preservation. As an adult she left the advantages of urban living and moved to the Standing Rock Reservation—the open prairies of her roots—even though her arduous travel schedule was made more difficult by this relocation to the rural prairies of South Dakota. During her lifetime, she and Sitting Bull were listed by a South Dakota Department of Tourism brochure as the two most outstanding Sioux Indians.[2] The list of her many accomplishments is long and varied. She was awarded the prestigious MacArthur Fellowship (also known as the MacArthur Genius Award), served as the first American Indian elected as a senior officer of the National Spiritual Assembly of the Bahá'ís of the United States, was elected chair of the Indigenous Women's Conference in Beijing, and was posthumously inducted to the National Women's Hall of Fame. She accomplished so much while being a devoted mother and grandmother. In addition, she was well-known for taking in stray dogs and feeding anyone who showed up at her door.

II

The Early Years

Pat was born in Pocatello, Idaho on January 21, 1928. At the time of her birth, her father was a clerk for the Bureau of Indian Affairs (BIA), and her mother was a nurse for the Indian Health Service (IHS). They were stationed at Fort Hall, Idaho. Her younger sister, Frances (Milligan), was born two and a half years later on November 3, 1930.

As a result of her father working for the BIA, the family moved frequently. BIA housing was usually close to the offices for the convenience of the employees. The result was that the girls did not mingle much with children from the Reservations. There is no indication that Pat had any enduring friendships from her childhood days. Her children and grandchildren recall that most of her early day recollections were about her parents and her sister. Her son Kevin said she was generally known as a BIA brat, the common term for the children of government employees living on the Reservations.

When Pat and her sister were too young to go to school, their working parents found a reliable and responsible person to take care of them. He was a Shoshone medicine man named Tagwits. Pat recalled an incredible story from these early years. One day their mother had prepared some soup for Tagwits and he was peacefully enjoying it when the over-tired little girls, sitting on the floor, started fussing. Tagwits tapped on the table and sang. As he sang a broom in the corner of the room danced about the room in time with the singing. The girls stared at the dancing broom. They reached out to grab it, but the broom would dance away. Laughter quickly replaced whining for the girls. With their mood change the broom danced back to its corner and Tagwits finished his soup.

Years later, Pat credited the dancing broom for her ability to accept the possibilities of the unbelievable. She felt she never had to suspend belief or intellect to accept the incredible.[3] It also established a life-long belief in the power of transformation. Here, from the inanimate to the animate. From this experience, watching a wooden broom come to life, she was led to a question that resonated throughout her life: What are the limits for change?

The family went to the Catholic Church regularly, but Indian ways were at the heart of the girls' upbringing. Traditional Lakota values were stressed, as well as the need to get valuable skills for success in the white man's world.

When Pat was about six years old, she entered an interpretive dance competition and won a trip to the national event at an exposition in Chicago. Pat, her mother, and Frances took the train from Pocatello to Chicago. She did not win anything, but she reported that the experience was priceless. Being an independent spirit, she wandered away from her hotel and got lost in the big city. With composure, this six-year-old approached a cab driver and told him what hotel she was staying at and that he should take her there and get paid by her mother when they arrived, which the cab driver did!

Her poor mother was frantic when she couldn't find her daughter. In desperation, she called Pat's father, and it was no small matter to make a long-distance telephone call in 1933. Pat then walked in, confident and unperturbed. Her parents' training in independence and resourcefulness paid off and set the pattern for her future: without resources, but with resourcefulness and confidence, Pat would find ways to achieve her goals.

The family was closely knit. Eva generally had a garden and the girls would help with the weeding and other gardening tasks. The girls remembered fondly the picnics and camping trips they would go on. John often took the girls to baseball games. He had a big St. Bernard dog, Patty, who was a favorite of the girls. John made a harness for Patty, who would pull the girls on a sled over the snow. They would have great fun romping together.

Education was also important to Pat's parents. Books were a prominent fixture in their home, and the *New Yorker* magazine could always be found in the living room.* A love for books was something that was instilled in Pat from an early age, and remained with her for life.

Their parents wanted the best for the girls so they could function well in both the Indian world and the dominant society. Both girls were given elocution and declamation lessons to help prepare them for the outside world. Traditions were also emphasized, however, and Pat's mother made her a buckskin dress. She taught the girls to hoop dance and they also took ballet lessons.

Eva's father's name was Noel. His personal Indian name was; "Makȟókiŋyaŋ," a

Pat with her beloved grandfather.

contraction of two words; "Makȟá" (earth), and "Okíŋyaŋ" (flying on or over)—he who flies over or on the earth. He was also known as Little Crow and often lived with the family. He would tell the girls many stories. The girls learned much of the Lakota values and rites on their grandfather's knees. While they attended and respected the

---

* Books were important to her throughout her entire life. Her granddaughter, Maymangwa, cataloged several hundred in her personal collection, and she was a frequent patron at the Mobridge library.

teachings of the Catholic Church, the girls learned there was really no division between the sacred and the secular and that the spiritual world was not just inside a building. They learned that no matter what anyone is doing in life, sacred elements are involved.

Pat and Frances were taught the real meaning of being a warrior, although that term can be misleading. Europeans used the word "warrior" for people they fought against throughout the world. Among the Lakota, the men who went into battle were known as the *akicita* (akíčhita), which does not have a direct translation. It means, "one who has given up his own ego and devotes his life to the betterment and protection of the community." Being an akicita was like being part of an altruistic service organization. This was called the *okolakiciye* (okȟólakičhiye). For instance, when the village had to move, the okolakiciye directed the operation. They led in the hunt and took care of the widows, the elderly, and the infirm. They were the social welfare network for the village. They lived the Lakota values. Naturally, when the village was under attack, the akicita became the soldiers in the first line of defense. This function of defense was a last resort and is what the invading white culture often encountered. As a result non-Indians saw only this limited role and assumed they were like army soldiers whose primary purpose was battle. So, they called them warriors. In truth, fighting was the akicita's role out of reluctant necessity.

The girls soaked up these and many other stories from their grandfather. They also had living examples to look up to in the lives of their parents and grandfather, who reflected Lakota values in their lives. These became crucial elements in the formation of Pat and Frances' attitudes toward life and their worldviews.

Since both parents worked, Pat, being the older sister, took a protective role in looking after her younger sister. Pat nicknamed Frances "Weewee" or "Fran." And Frances, recalling those days, said of Pat—she called her Patsy—"She was my big sister and she kind of looked after me—dominated me really and I loved her very much. We had a marvelous childhood."[4] They played Monopoly and other children's games, and they played tennis, which was especially encouraged as their father had been a championship tennis player in his youth. They also went skiing and swimming, loved the outdoors, and generally enjoyed their early years.

For a time, while living in Arizona, the girls went to a boarding school. Fran reported that when they were at the boarding school she was about five years old, the youngest person there, and they had a lot of chores to do that were hard for her. She could not do them all, so her big sister would come to her rescue. She would help with some chores and do others. Fran said: "She was so good to me. . . . The nuns were quite strict, and she would just help me out. She took care of me; her little sister."[5]

This protective attitude was entrenched for life. As an adult, Pat would take care of and do the chores for those who were less able. Even more, she would look for ways that people could overcome obstacles themselves. It was not her way to complain, feel burdened, or put upon. It was just that when someone needed help, she was there.

Doing well in school was important and the girls were given money for good grades even though the family income was only fourteen dollars every two weeks. Students with the best grades were allowed to sit in the front row of the class and that is what the girls were taught to strive for.

During the three years the family lived near the Klamath Agency in Oregon, Pat was encouraged to read all of the books in the school library. She started with book titles at the beginning of the alphabet and read all the way through Z. This was the beginning of her dedication to lifelong learning.

One time, while the family was living on the Colorado River Tribes Reservation near Parker, Arizona, their mother gave the girls some money to go to a movie. When they came home Eva asked them about the movie. They said they weren't able to see it because all the Indians had to sit in the back of the theater and they were too small to see over the people in front of them. With righteous indignation, Eva took the girls back to the movie theater and confronted the manager, telling him that he had better treat her daughters with respect and let them sit where they wanted or she would have all the Indians in the area boycott his theater. The girls were never again treated with disrespect in that movie theater. It was an example Pat would emulate all her life. As problems arose, she would unhesitatingly go to whoever was responsible and confront the problem directly, seeking a resolution. She also distinguished between the problem and the individual responsible.

When Pat was about nine years old, her parents asked a Nez Percé woman to teach Pat the 23rd Psalm of David in Indian sign language. The 23rd Psalm was a major element in convincing Indians that the "black coats" (Catholic priests) could also be spiritual. So they sat in a Walgreen's drugstore dining area, and Pat was taught the Indian sign language for this psalm. The waitress, assuming they were deaf and communicating in American Sign Language, approached Pat's mother and asked, "And what do they want?"

American Indian sign language had developed to help different tribes communicate with each other. While most of the hundreds of verbal languages of North American Indians were mutually unintelligible, there were two forms of common communications. One was cryptographic, many samples of which are found in caves throughout the continent. The other was sign language. Both of these forms were used to share ideas, tell of dangers, and give information that was important in hunting and commerce.

Pat's oral translation of the Indian sign language version of the 23rd Psalm is as follows: "The great Father above is the shepherd Chief. I'm his and with Him I want not. He throws out to me a rope and the name of the rope is love and He draws me and He draws me and He draws me to a place where the grass is green and the water is good and I eat and I lay down satisfied. Sometime, it may be very soon, it may be a long, long time, when the shepherd chief will draw me to a place between mountains. It is dark there, but I'll draw back not, I'll be afraid not for it is there between these mountains that He will meet me. Sometimes, He makes the love rope into a whip. Then, afterwards He gives me a staff to lean upon. He spread before me a table with all kinds of food. He puts His Hands upon my head and all the tired is gone. My cup He fills until it runs over. What I tell you is true. I lie not, for these paths lead to the big tepee, where dwells the shepherd Chief, and when I die I will live with Him forever."

During the same time, Pat's father wanted her to learn classical guitar. So he talked to an internationally renowned classical guitar player and paid him to give Pat ten guitar lessons. He could only afford ten, but he wanted to do what he could. She was also given lessons in both Spanish and Hawaiian dancing. Later in life, she gave lessons in these skills to supplement the family income.

During vacation times, the family would travel to visit the Standing Rock Reservation in North and South Dakota (home of their mother), the White Earth Reservation in Minnesota (home of their father), or travel to Canada where many of their father's relatives had moved to escape repressive policies against American Indians. A friend of Pat's, Jacqueline Left Hand Bull, feels that this early travel provided Pat with a poise and sophistication that was a hallmark of her life.[6]

Their father's final working years were at the Indian School in Riverside, California. After retirement the family moved to Alhambra, California, where Pat graduated from high school.

It was while she was a teenager in the Los Angeles area that she probed further into the Catholic Church. She had been asking the nuns and priests where the Pope got his authority. She knew that, for the Lakota, the Sacred Pipe was a tangible symbol of the covenant with the Great Spirit through the White Buffalo Calf Maiden. She wanted to know the covenantal basis for the Pope. The answers she got from the nuns and priests were basically that she must accept this on faith. This was not sufficient for Pat. She was referred to the bishop, who lived some distance away.

She saved up her money from babysitting and ironing and rode on a bus for several hours to reach the address given to her, where she could meet with the bishop. Even though she had an appointment with the bishop the receptionist told her to wait, which she did for many hours. Finally, everyone was leaving for the day and she still hadn't been called. She saw the bishop leaving his office and she approached him and said she had a question. The bishop said, "Oh, yes. What was your question?"

Pat asked where the authority for the Pope came from. The bishop said, "Oh, young lady, I've heard about you. I'm sorry, but if you pursue this line of questioning I will have no recourse but to excommunicate you."[7] That was the end of her being a Catholic.

After high school, she attended the John Muir College in Pasadena and later transferred to the University of California in Los Angeles (UCLA). This was in the late 1940s and Pat reported that she was the only Indian attending UCLA, and that there were only six Indians in all of the colleges in the United States at that time. There was a lot of open prejudice against American Indians, creating severe disadvantages. Therefore, she would often say she was Hawaiian in order to go places where Indians were not allowed.

Her earlier swimming lessons paid off when she attended UCLA. She became a member of the women's aquatic ballet team and taught swimming at the local YMCA. She has said of those years that she was also frivolous and loved to dance.[8] Unfortunately, she left no details of her frivolous youth—that is left up to your imagination.

Funds for college were limited. She only had two changes of clothes, and giving swimming lessons provided her with valuable cash. As a result, her grades suffered and she was placed on academic probation. In June of 1950 she was suspended from UCLA, but readmitted on probation in October. Hard work enabled her to regain her good standing and she earned an interdepartmental degree in English, Anthropology, Geology, and Physical Education. Then she took education courses that would qualify her to teach.

Her experience in college, especially her struggle to earn enough money to pay for her education, was an example of her tenacity and perseverance. During these difficult years she showed that she could also enjoy life in the midst of struggles. She was in an environment that was hostile rather than supportive of Indians; there were no other Native Americans on campus with whom she could commiserate; and she had to work to earn her way. Her rewards, from the standpoint of grades, were mediocre. Anyone of lesser mettle would have given up. It is an enormous tribute to Pat's fortitude that she persisted and later returned to UCLA to earn a Master's Degree in Public Administration and still later to teach there.

Among the results of that experience was the strong desire that her children and grandchildren get an education, but not have to work their way through as she did. She also wanted Indian youngsters to study in their own familiar environment, learning and applauding their own culture and traditions and not having the pressure of cultural challenges. Many young Indians have certain responsibilities—such as caring for aging parents or grandparents—that are considered essential and cannot be fulfilled if they go away to college. They would have to choose between a college education and fulfilling family responsibilities. Most Indian youngsters would put the needs of the family above an education. There, the early seeds of Pat's future commitment to establishing colleges on the Reservations were planted.

Before getting into her work on behalf of colleges on Reservations, however, it is important to know more about Pat's heritage.

III

Heritage[9]

Pat's family came from a number of distinct tribes. Because of this, she grew up viewing all mankind as members of the same family. Her mother, Eva Flying Earth McGillis, had ancestors from a number of Sioux bands—both Dakota and Lakota, which are both Sioux. This ancestry includes Hunkpapa (Húŋkpapȟa), Ihanktonwan (Iháŋktȟuŋwaŋ), and Mdewakantonwan (Bdewákhaŋthuŋwaŋ) Santee. Her father, John McGillis, was from the Mississippi band of Chippewa, also known as Ojibway or Anishnabe.

Ironically, the name *Sioux* is said to be derived from a Chippewa word meaning sneaky, crafty, snake-like, or small rattlesnake. Some scholars, however, claim it is an Algonquin word, relayed by French-Canadian trappers, that means "Northern Iroquoian" or simply "people who speak a different language." Because of the negative connotation of the word *Sioux,* the people generally prefer to be called Lakota or Dakota. The preferred term means *ally* or *friendly person* and has the connotation of being connected spiritually—a friend on a deep and profound level.

The girls' parents felt it was important that they learn the moral values and wisdom that is part of Indian culture, as well as the ways of the dominant culture. The girls were encouraged to be Indians at the most basic level. At the same time, skills were needed to function in society. But these skills were to be learned and used on a superficial level and not internalized. The intrinsic part of their being would be Indian. Both the Lakota and Chippewa are matrilineal so a greater part of the influence on Pat's life was from the Lakota side.

Pat's maternal great grandfather was Chief Little Crow (circa 1810–1863). His Indian name was Taoyate Duta (Thaóyate Dúta), meaning "His Red Nation." He is better known as Little Crow, (Kȟaŋǧí Čík'ala). This name probably comes from a poor translation of his father's name, Cetan Wakuwa Mani (Čhetáŋ Wakhúwa Máni). A more appropriate translation would be "The Hawk that Hunts While Walking" or, less accurate but still used, "Charging Hawk." Three generations of the family carried the name; Khaŋǧí Čík'ada (Little Crow) in addition to their own personal names.

He was chief of the Mdewakanton Dakota band, who were living in the southwest area of what is now known as Minnesota. He was elected as the Dakota spokesman for negotiating and signing the Treaty of Fort Laramie in 1851.[10]* Seven years later, in 1858, he went to Washington, D.C. in an unsuccessful attempt to get the government to honor the treaty. It is reported that he had a meeting with President James Buchanan in his failed attempt to get justice for his people.

There had been 150 years of peaceful living with whites in the Minnesota Territory, and Little Crow desired to maintain good relations. He tried to get along with the customs of the United States,

---

* For the whites, the purpose of the two-week-long negotiations was to provide safe passage for wagon trains on their westward trek. For the Indians, there was a desire to preserve their mode of living and survive amidst the deluge of white people. The white negotiators felt they got the concessions they wanted for the price of "just a few blankets and some promises." The promises included a guarantee for perpetuity to Indian ownership of the Black Hills in general and Mt. Rushmore in particular. These had been held as sacred for centuries. Now that sacred spot has the graven images of four U.S. presidents, each one of whom would be accused of human rights abuses or crimes against humanity by today's standards. Other promises included perpetual and unlimited hunting rights in the Dakotas, Wyoming, and Montana, and government provisions. From the outset, the government did little to live up to the terms of the treaty. Ultimately, all the Indians got for their concessions were "a few blankets" and broken promises.

replacing his Native clothing with trousers and jackets with brass buttons, joining the Episcopal Church, and taking up farming.

For four years after his return from Washington, he saw that the government would not honor its agreements. He saw the plight of his people as the treaties were broken, more and more land was taken by settlers, and game became scarce from over-hunting. For the most part, the Indians were friendly and hospitable, but the large numbers of whites moving in strained resources. Few of the whites even respected, let alone assimilated, into the local traditions. They insisted on their own religion and way of life. The Dakota worried that the increasing number of new settlers would overrun the established cultures and lifestyle of the Indians in the area.*

Little Crow pleaded for peace, seeing the unstoppable coming of the white man. He was called a coward for not fighting, and he replied, "Taoyate Duta (speaking of himself) is not a coward, and he is not a fool! . . . You are full of the white man's devil water (alcohol). You are like dogs in the Hot Moon when they run mad and snap at their own shadows. . . . Kill one–two–ten (the white men), and ten times ten will come to kill you. Count your fingers all day long and white men with guns in their hands will come faster than you can count."[11] The pressure from his people was strong. Reluctantly, he gave in to take up arms in an attempt to force the government to honor its treaties.

On August 4, 1862, about five hundred Dakota Indians broke into the food warehouses at the government facility called the Lower Agency. In an attempt to regain peace, the agent in charge, Thomas Galbraith, wisely ordered defending troops not to shoot. Instead he called for a conference to resolve the issues. At the conference, Little Crow pointed out that they were owed money to buy food and warned that, "When men are hungry, they help them-

---

* The same concerns are voiced today by white Christians in the United States who complain about Latinos, Muslims, and other groups of people. Many forefathers of today's whites, who arrived during earlier times, would be called illegal immigrants today.

selves." A trader at the conference, Andrew Myrick, replied, "So far as I am concerned, if they are hungry let them eat grass or their own dung."[12]

This set off the Dakota uprising of 1862, which is also known as the Minnesota uprising—Dakota referring to the people, and Minnesota referring to the area in which the uprising took place. Little Crow is best known as the leader of the uprising. This was the first of a series of battles that raged over the next thirty years involving various bands of Sioux. Probably the best known battle was the Wounded Knee Massacre on December 30, 1890. The final campaign was at Pine Ridge, South Dakota in January 1891.

As for Little Crow, on July 3, 1863, he and his son were picking berries about twelve miles from Hutchinson, Minnesota. A farmer, Nathan Lampson, and his son saw them. In order to collect the bounty being paid for Indian scalps, the Lampsons shot and killed Little Crow. After he was shot, Little Crow told his twelve-year-old son to run for his life, which he did. Lampson was given an extra $500 bonus (roughly $52,000 today) when authorities discovered that he had killed Little Crow.

There is a small monument on a farm outside Hutchinson, Minnesota near where Little Crow was shot. It has no reference to him, but mentions some of the European settlers who were involved with the skirmishes of the time. On the bank of the Crow River, in a park next to a bridge over the river, there is a statue of Little Crow looking up the Crow River. Nearby, a commemorative plaque reads, "He fought for the Indian's right to live in peace in this land."

Five and a half months after Little Crow was killed, on the day after Christmas, December 26, 1863, President Abraham Lincoln signed an executive order that called for the execution of thirty-eight Dakota Indians in Minnesota.

Following Little Crow's murder, Pat's grandfather, Noel, his brother, John—both called "Little Crow"—and many other Dakota Indians fled from what is now Minnesota. Many went to Canada and others went to the Lakota country in what was then called the Dakota Territory. John settled near Cannonball in the northern part

Statue of Chief Little Crow looking up the Crow River in Hutchinson, Minnesota

of what is now the Standing Rock Reservation, and Noel settled near Wakpala in a spot known as Flying Earth bottom along the Grand River. It was there that he met and married Pat's grandmother Agnes, a Hunkpapa Lakota.*

---

* The Hunkpapa are one of seven Lakota bands. The name means "Gatekeepers" or "Head of the Circle," and is based on the tradition of the Hunkpapa in setting up their lodges at the entryway to the circle of the Great Council when tribes met in convocation.

The name Flying Earth invokes the spirit of rising above material attachments and soaring in the realm that knows no limitations. Noel and Agnes Flying Earth had a ranch and many cattle. Noel was renowned for his wisdom and generosity, regularly feeding the poor and taking care of those in need. Although such generosity might sound surprising to many in the dominant culture, in most so-called "primitive societies" the honor and prestige of strong leaders is based on how well they care for those in need. While Noel understood English, for reasons that are not hard to imagine, he refused to speak it.

Pat's mother, Eva, was born and raised on the ranch, which she loved and she spoke of often. She had a favorite horse and would ride throughout the area in the early years of the twentieth century. She was highly respected as an outstanding rider. Sadly, in 1918 the Spanish flu epidemic killed most of the family. Eva and her brother Joe were the only children who survived.

Education was important to the Flying Earth family. Eva's mother and father were both eager that she get as much education as she could. That meant leaving home and going to school elsewhere. Her education away from home started at Haskell Institute* in Lawrence, Kansas, and she got her nurses training in Minneapolis. During her school years she met a handsome young man, John McGillis, from the White Earth Reservation in Minnesota.

John was not a Lakota but a Chippewa.† The legendary feud between the two tribes had gone on for generations. But, as with Ro-

---

* Now known as Haskell Indian Nations University.

† Pat usually used the term *Anishnabe*. She and her children, Kevin and Winona, refer to themselves as Lakota. However, Pat's niece, Sheridan MacKnight, refers to herself as Chippewa or Chippewa / Sioux because the Chippewa nation paid for her art training. Her stated goal is that her work do honor to the Chippewa nation that made her career possible. Every year Sheridan participates in the Indian Art Festival in Santa Fe, New Mexico. She does her work on ledger paper because in the early days that was the only paper Indians could use for their art. Her work is sold through the leading galleries of Santa Fe. See her Web Site: www.SheridanMacKnight.com.

meo and Juliet, tribal difference did not interfere with love, and these two, from hostile backgrounds, got married.

John's grandfather was Scotch-Irish and married a Chippewa—John's grandmother. He attended Haskell and from there went to Pennsylvania, where he joined the staff of the Carlisle Indian Industrial School. At Carlisle he became an assistant to the famous football coach "Pop" Warner. Being a stellar athlete, he was on the team even though he was a staff member. The legendary Jim Thorpe was one of his teammates. A 2007 *Sports Illustrated* article called the Carlisle team of that period "The Team that Invented Football."

John loved to tell the story of two Pueblo Indians who were attending Carlisle. The Pueblos were noted as great runners. They were not competitive, but did it simply for the love of running. There was a track and field event pitting Carlisle against Pennsylvania State College. In a foot race, the two Pueblo students were far ahead of the others. In order not to compete with each other, the two of them fell into lock step so they would finish in a tie, well ahead of the rest.

Carlisle played a contentious role in the history of Indian education. Many Indian children were taken from their families living on the newly formed Indian Reservations in order to attend school. Carlisle was expected to transform them into docile tailors, bakers, and farmworkers. The school was founded by Captain Richard Henry Pratt in 1879 as a deliberate effort to forcibly assimilate—or "civilize"—American Indian children. During its thirty-nine years of existence (1879–1918) Carlisle had enrolled approximately 10,000 children. Of these, eight percent graduated while more than twice that number ran away.

Pratt had earned a reputation for getting concessions from tribal leaders by his treatment of hostages during the so-called "Indian Wars." His technique was to use intimidation, cutting of long hair, dressing Indians in military uniforms, prohibiting the use of Indian languages, forbidding the practice of Indian religions, separation from family and home areas, and other procedures that would be considered torture today. His stated intent was to "Kill the Indian and save the man." He applied this same philosophy to the children at Carlisle. One historian noted that "Pratt saw his education program with the Native Americans as analogous to his domestication of wild turkeys."[13]*

This kind of thinking and treatment of Indians has and continues to cause a multitude of problems that Pat spent her life correcting. It may be said that Pat devoted her life to reversing Pratt's creed. Rather than "Kill the Indian to save the man," her goal was the opposite. It could be described as: Let the Indian become himself to save the man, his culture, the country, and the world.

When the First World War broke out, John wanted to serve his country. At that time, Indians were not American citizens and were prohibited from serving in the armed forces. He protested and wrote letters that reached the upper echelons of the War Department. The policy was changed and he became the first American Indian to serve in the American armed forces. His home Reservation of White Earth, Minnesota boasted many World War I veterans, including at least one who played in John Philip Sousa's marching band. Still, citizenship was not granted to any of them until the Indian Citizenship Act of 1924. That was four years after women gained the right to vote. John's action opened the door to Indians in service and had a far-reaching effect. The heroic service of many Native American veterans in the First World War was a major factor in the passage of the Indian Citizenship Act.

After Eva and John were married in the late 1920s they began careers with the Bureau of Indian Affairs (BIA). John was an irrigation clerk and Eva was a nurse working for the Indian Health Service. This was a rarity. Few Indians were employed by government agencies, and for both husband wife to be employed was rarer still.

Pat learned French and Spanish in school, but, much to her sorrow, she learned neither Chippewa nor Lakota. Her father spoke

---

* More information can be found on the web by searching for "Carlisle Indian School Research Pages." Included on the web is a group photo of about 100 sad-faced young Carlisle students, all in uniforms with short haircuts.

Chippewa, but not Lakota. Her mother spoke Lakota, but not Chippewa, so the language of the home was English. She would hear the other languages when visitors came to visit her parents, but she reported that her proficiency in both was about that of a five or six year old. That may have influenced her passion for preserving Native languages. She often said the culture is in the language.

To give the girls a firm foundation in the Indian ways, they were often taken to ceremonies, such as the sun dance, even though all Indian rites were outlawed and both John and Eva could have been fired had their superiors known of this activity.* So, Indian worship was done in secret. As young as three, Pat was told not to tell anyone when the family went to Indian ceremonies. Even with their jobs on the line, the parents were determined that the girls learn the spiritual significance of the Indian ways. Some of Pat's most cherished childhood memories were going to Indian ceremonies and to her parent's home Reservation during vacation times. Her experiences on the Reservation entrenched even greater resolve in her work of preserving tribal languages and customs. She was determined to make it possible for Indian youth to find their way and be successful in the white man's world while also preserving their culture.

Fundamental to Lakota ways and the fiber of Reservation life is the story of the White Buffalo Calf Maiden,[14] whom the Lakota believe to be a Divine Messenger. Sometimes she is referred to as White Buffalo Calf Woman or White Buffalo Cow Woman or simply White Buffalo Calf. It is a story rich in symbolism and metaphor that highlights the dual nature of human beings. There are many minor variations of the story but the main elements are consistent. As an adult, Pat, together with two others, researched American Indian

---

* Indian religious ceremonies were outlawed by the U.S. Congress in 1904. Pat was among those who worked tirelessly for the passage of the American Indian Religious Freedom Act of 1978 to reverse that prohibition. Some of the language in that act came from her drafts. Today the sun dance is performed up to 200 times a year on various Reservations. Each sun dance Pat attended must have given her a special joy as her people could finally celebrate openly.

oral history and discovered twenty-three Individuals from different tribes who are considered by their tribes as Divine Messengers. Six of these were women. This is consistent both with Christ's statement in John 10:16 about other sheep and the Islamic tradition that 124,000 Messengers have been sent to mankind.

The story of White Buffalo Calf Maiden goes as follows: According to Pat, about 900 years ago (no exact date has been determined), at a time of famine, two young Teton* Indians were sent out as scouts in search of food. A terrible, unexpected storm came up followed by a sudden calm. Out of the calm a white buffalo calf came running toward them. The two young men discussed whether or not they should kill it for the meat. When they looked back, the calf had turned into the most beautiful woman they had ever seen, all clad in white. One young man, captivated by her beauty, had lascivious thoughts about her. She said: "Come, get what you want." And the licentious one rushed toward her. When he reached her, a black cloud engulfed them. When the cloud cleared, all that was left of the lustful young man were his bones. His companion fell to his knees and prayed for the spirit of his fallen brother. When he finished, the maiden told him that the other young man had become what he was seeking.

She told the scout(s) she came from Tȟuŋkášila, meaning *Grandfather* or the *Great Spirit*. Her reference to having been sent by "Grandfather" has been understood in various ways. Some people feel this refers to God. Other people maintain that God is so exalted as to be beyond direct communications. Therefore, intermediaries, Who reflect all the attributes of God, are used to convey divine messages. In this sense, the voice of "Grandfather" who sent the White Buffalo Calf Maiden could be the same voice that spoke to Moses in the Burning Bush, accompanied the dove as it descended to Christ at His baptism, and that spoke through Gabriel to Muhammad in the cave of Mount Hira. Muslims often refer to Muhammad as "Grandfather."

---

* Teton or Thítȟuŋwaŋ are other names for Lakota.

Then she spoke: "Don't be fearful, I am your older sister. Your grandfather above has authorized me to appear in His behalf because of His great love for His grandchildren. He has authorized me to present this message of love in the form of this counsel." She told the scout to return to his village and prepare for her coming. They were told to ". . . prepare a sacred space with some sage and spread it out on the ground and there I will present this message." She said she would come with a gift and a message. At that point she again became a white buffalo calf and scampered away.

There are many different ways to understand this story, but Kevin Locke shared his perspective. He said that a metaphorical understanding is that only one scout was looking for buffalo, which was the essence of physical sustenance as it provided meat, clothing, shelter, tools, and so on. When the young man met the maiden, instead of material gratification he received spiritual sustenance, which was far greater and more enduring than the mere physical. The pile of bones represents his being cleansed of his lower nature. He was so changed by this Holy Soul that when he returned to his village his transformation radiated to such an extent that the villagers immediately believed him and prepared for the coming of their guest.

However it is interpreted, the story continues with the village preparing for the coming of this unusual guest. A few days later a white buffalo calf came toward the village and, as she approached, she again turned into the beautiful woman, singing this song as she came closer:

With a visible breath I walk.
Towards a nation I walk.
With a visible voice I walk.
Something ancient, sacred and red I bring.*

---

* Niyáŋ tȟaŋíŋyaŋ mawáni ye / Oyáte waŋ imáwani / Ho tȟaŋíŋyaŋ mawáni ye / Walúta waŋ awáu we.

She told them she would only be with them for four days to convey a message and a gift. The message included the fact that they must change their ways. She talked to the men, women, and children separately, telling each about the importance of unity and that all must work together for the good of the nation.

One interpretation is that even though the message was intended for one group of people, suited to their capacity and understanding of that time, it contains timeless references that are consistent with revelations given to other people. Her teachings spoke of peace and unity, and the Lakota tried to implement that when white men came, but there were too many barriers to overcome. The births of white buffalo calves in recent years is seen by some Lakota as a time of fulfillment when there will be appreciation of other ways, people can truly be united, and those barriers will be overcome.

Previous to the coming of White Buffalo Calf Maiden, the Lakota had been a warring people. They were taught that they must now strive for peace. Her teachings are remembered through seven sacred rites, three basic principles, and four core values.

She gave them the sacred pipe, symbolizing the promise as a covenant until the return of the Spirit. She explained that the bowl, made of red pipestone, represented the earth, which is their mother and grandmother. The stem, made of wood, represents men and everything that grows on the earth. When the two pieces come together, it symbolizes Creation. She said when they smoke the pipe they should lift it up in thanks to the Creator and the prayers of thanksgiving would ascend with the smoke. They should also cover themselves and each other with its smoke as if receiving a blessing. She said it was the pipe of peace and truth. When sharing the pipe, men must have peace in their hearts and speak the truth. The pipe is physical evidence of the covenant that links the people with the Great Spirit and the practice of sacred rites. The pipe still exists today. The nineteenth keeper of the pipe lives on the Cheyenne River Reservation in South Dakota.*

---

* Many Caucasians refer to this as a peace pipe since whenever they were invited to smoke the pipe, it was seen as a gesture of friendship and peace. Most white men failed to see any significance to the ritual as a means for spiritual cleansing and

At the end of the fourth day, the beautiful maiden said she would come again. That is, there would be a new message from "Grandfather." That time would bring peace and the people of the world would learn to love one another and be united. Then she turned into a red buffalo calf, then a brown one, and later became a white buffalo calf. Still later she again became a black buffalo. This buffalo bowed to the four corners of the universe and disappeared over a hill. Some Lakota interpret this to mean that at the time of return all races will be united.

On rare occasions the birth of a white buffalo calf has been recorded. In recent years, on August 20, 1994 a white buffalo calf was born near Janesville, Wisconsin. Another one was born in 1996 in South Dakota. A third one was born in August, 2006. Many Lakota believe this means that her prophecy will soon be fulfilled.

Three Principles

The first of the three principles is illustrated with the Lakota word "wakan yeja (wakȟáŋyeža)." That is the word for child, but translated literally it means "sacred being." This concept serves as the frame of reference for parents, educators, and helping professionals everywhere and is a fundamental Lakota principle and tradition.

Another of these core principles is "mitakuye oyasin (Mitákuye Oyás'iŋ)." The first word refers to "my relatives" and the second means "everyone." As Pat has explained, "everything in the world is sacred: the two-legged, the four-legged, the winged creatures, the crawling ones, the finned ones, and the rooted ones."[15] This includes things underwater, on the land, the sky above, and plants and animals—all are related and have an impact on one another.

The third core concept—Wolakota (Wólakȟota)—is commonly translated as "peace" with the connotation of harmony. It is a view

---

renewal. General Custer was invited to a ceremony one time. He was told to have peace in his heart or suffer the consequences. When he returned to his camp he told his fellow officers that he was not impressed. Soon thereafter, he rode with his troops over that same area, slaughtering the people who were there. This was shortly before Custer was killed at the battle of the Little Big Horn in Montana.

that life requires balance among all things. Inner confusion and chaos is the result of a life out of balance.

Seven Rituals

The seven rituals and ceremonies, such as the sun dance and other ceremonies, reflect White Buffalo Calf Maiden teachings that are for the purpose of spiritual cleansing, reestablishing and maintaining that fundamental balance, and being in harmony with all that is.[16]

The others are: purification (the sweat lodge, inípi); releasing of the soul (wanáǧi yuškápi)—a grieving rite for the departed one year after passing; becoming a woman (išnáthi awíčhalowaŋpi); the vision quest for young men (haŋbléčheyapi); making a relative (huŋkáyapi)—adoption of those who have lost a loved one; and tossing the ball (tȟápa waŋkáyeyapi)—a process for selecting people given special responsibility for protecting the environment.

Each of the rituals has special importance, but a word more should be said about the sun dance (wí wáŋyaŋg wačhípi—they dance gazing at the sun). It has been called a "festival of prayer." The complex procedures are reverently executed and it is rich with symbolism. Black Elk claimed it was one of the Lakota's greatest rites.* Attending the sun dance was a high priority for Pat. It can well be imagined that she would think of her childhood and the many times the family would sneak away to remote areas because the ritual was outlawed. It is ironic that the ceremony, which was dedicated to purification and hope for world peace and unity, was outlawed and could only be performed in secret. Since its legalization by the American Indian Religious Freedom Act of 1978, the sun dance has enjoyed great resurgence.

The dancers do not dance for themselves, but on behalf of some other person. They dance, fast, pray, and endure pain and deprivation for four days to demonstrate their willingness to sacrifice for the good of the whole. It is a reflection of a basic Lakota concept that the

---

*See *The Sacred Pipe*, p. 67

good of the group is far more important than concern for oneself. A tree, placed in the middle of the sacred arena, is called the "Tree of Life"—by its very name it is linked with worldwide spiritual symbolism. Throughout the four days of prayer and fasting, the dancers fulfill their tasks with a humble attitude of sacrifice and courage in praise of the Great Spirit, commitment to the ultimate fulfillment of White Buffalo Calf Maiden's prophecies, and dedicated service to their communities. Missionaries claimed it was devil worship and were successful in having it and other rituals outlawed. As a small child, Pat loved the ceremony. As an adult, each time she attended the sun dance she was revitalized in her work for the rights of all people.

The seven rituals and three core principles underpin the four main Lakota values: courage, respect, generosity, and wisdom.

Lakota Values

One time Pat heard a panel discussion by a group of sociologists talking about the primary values of the dominant North American culture—not the lofty and often maudlin stated values found in political speeches, sermons, graduation ceremonies, or the media, but the real values that people live by. The sociologists agreed there were three core values in mainstream America: mercantilism or commercialism, acquisitiveness, and individualism. This honest look at the American value system had a major impact on Pat's thinking. She thought of how these mainstream American values contrasted so starkly with the age-old Lakota ways.

While trade had long been practiced among the Lakota, it was incidental barter rather than a basic and intense part of life. The idea of personal profit did not exist. Harmony with other people, within one's self, and with everything in existence was fundamental to one's life. Commercial interests were, at best, secondary.

Instead of acquiring things, generosity is a prized Lakota value. Accumulating things, living in a big house, or driving a fancy car are not important. Sharing and relationships are most important.

While individuals are all considered sacred, for the Lakota the needs of the community take precedence over personal desires and needs. For one to have more than enough while others are in want is incomprehensible.

Pat expressed sincere regret that the values dominant in mainstream America, so at odds with Lakota morals, cause so much conflict and confusion for youngsters today. Lakota children are taught generosity (wówačhaŋtognaka), bravery (wóohitika), respect (ohóla), and wisdom (wóksape). At the same time, in the outside world, on television and in schools, they find a culture that honors and encourages a self-centered individualism, acquisitiveness, and commercialism as primary values. Indoctrination in this materialist outlook begins at an early age. All three values are taught in the annual North American ritual of taking children to department stores and malls to tell Santa Claus what they want for Christmas. The North American style of children's birthday parties reinforces self-centeredness and these material values. The attitude of "What's in it for me?" and the "me generation" should come as no surprise. Frustration over conflicting worldviews seems inevitable and puts noncompetitive Indian children at a severe disadvantage in such a highly competitive world.

The first of the four Lakota values, courage or fortitude, is so important that it relates directly to survival. It is the strength of character that equips people to meet and survive danger and troubles. One special group is referred to as "bravehearted women." A story Pat often heard and loved to relate was of a battle in which the bravehearted women were on their ponies at the edge of the battlefield seeking ways to be of service. One young woman saw her brother fall when his horse was shot out from under him. Instantly, she rode into the heat of battle leaning low over the side of her horse. Zigzagging to avoid cavalry bullets, she reached for her brother and helped him on her horse and then rode beyond the battle's edge. White recorded history refers to it as the "Battle of the Rosebud." Indian oral history calls it the "Battle When the Girl Saved Her Brother."

Pat has often said that in modern times courage is needed to distinguish between right and wrong, true and false, and to act on that knowledge. It requires seeing with one's own eyes and not through the eyes of others. There are many bravehearted women today. They are the mothers raising their children in impoverished circumstances with little hope for relief. They are also attorneys, doctors, judges, and others. In addition to whatever else they are doing, they fight for better housing, health programs, and the rights of their people.

The second value, respect, literally means "to address a relative." Respect is embedded in the language. In addition to the natural parents, the terms "father" and "mother" may be applied to aunts and uncles or other close adults. This builds a protective web of extended family. Marriage is not only between the man and woman, but unites two families.

An outstanding example of the strength of this attitude was shown when there was a murder in a village. The younger relatives of the murdered man wanted a suitable punishment. A wiser elder listened to their views and challenged them to choose the hard way, one that would put out the fire in everyone's heart. The elder responded: "Was the dead your brother? Then this man shall be your brother. Or your uncle? Or your cousin? As for me, he was my nephew; and so this man shall be my nephew." The murderer was brought to the council and offered a peace pipe and the elder said: "Smoke now with these your new relatives, for they have chosen to take you to themselves in place of one who is not here." With this, tears trickled down the murderer's face. He had been trapped by loving, respectful kinship.[17]

This respect implies a special level of trust in talking with family members, and goes even further. Since all living things are related, it includes a respectful attitude toward all creation. The entire world is seen as an interconnected network. How you think about and treat other people, creatures, and the environment reflects back on you. Treating anything disrespectfully really says you do not have much respect for yourself. The attitude of respect elevates special occasions, such as prayer or smoking the sacred pipe, to the highest level of reverence for the Creator.

The third core value, generosity, concerns not only material possessions but also food, time, and experience. It is closely related to compassion. Children are taught this from earliest childhood. Without asking, the best food or other goods is simply placed before a visitor. When children are caught sharing and exhibiting other forms of generosity and compassion, their parents praise them.

Pat mentioned one time when there were a number of guests at a sweat ceremony and a stew was prepared for sharing afterward. While the elders were in the sweat lodge, some of the younger ones ate all of the meat out of the stew. The guests received the leftovers. Out of earshot of the guests, Pat spoke to the youngsters who had eaten the meat. There were no remonstrations or berating of the children for what they did. She simply told them that taking the best for themselves and leaving the leftovers for the guests makes people think you do not respect them. No more was said and it never happened again.

A sacred rite related to generosity is "Preparing a Girl for Womanhood." The rite is for a young girl who has just started menstruating. Usually the oldest woman of the family selects four women from the community who are highly respected for living up to Lakota values. The selected women and the girl go into a tent. The women wash the girl with sage water, and then each of the older women shares her experience of becoming a Lakota woman. They explain what is expected of the young girl, how she should behave, and what she should look for in selecting a husband. Whenever Pat was in the tent with a young girl, she would tell the girl to consider the eagle. When it is time to mate, the female picks up a stick in her beak and flies high, dropping it for her suitor to catch in mid air. Then she gets a larger stick and repeats it until the stick is quite large. When she finds a suitor who can catch a big stick, she is ready to mate knowing that when an eaglet falls out of the nest, her mate will be able to retrieve it. A bowl of water is offered to the young girl three times. Only on the fourth offering may she drink. The same thing is done with dried buffalo meat. She is told that only after she has given drink and fed those who thirst or are hungry can she partake herself. When they emerge from the tent, they find much of the village gathered around, welcoming this girl into womanhood. Then there will be a feast in her honor including a giveaway, which involves giving gifts to others, usually of blankets.

The fourth value is wisdom, which is to be sought and gained over the course of one's entire life. It is not focused on material things or on earning a living, but has to do with understanding the meaning within the natural patterns of life; living spiritual values and knowing the design and purpose of life; and appreciating dreams—of both the day and the night. Again there is a special ceremony to recognize the importance of gaining wisdom. For young men it is the vision quest. When embarking on their vision quest, young men go off by themselves to pray and fast for four days in order to seek direction for their lives. The quest for a vision does not always work the first time. Pat said she knew one young man who went on his quest once a year for eleven years until he finally got his directions. When the young man returns he cannot impose his new understanding and insights on others. Whatever he learned is considered private. It is an important key for starting a life in search of wisdom. This continued quest for understanding and wisdom is one of the reasons why Lakota elders are venerated rather than marginalized, and why their company and companionship is sought and cherished by the young.

In later life, when Pat would make presentations before a white audience about Indian matters, she would acknowledge that on most Reservations only about one third of the people follow traditional ways. But there is so much to learn from these traditions, and few people of the dominant society have contact with Indians who follow the traditional ways, and many are not even aware of their existence. Most of the impressions formed about Indians come from movies, television, and those they see living on the fringe of societies. The negative accounts of Indians who have gotten into trouble, as reported on the evening news and newspapers, add to negative perceptions of Indians. Pat spent her life addressing these misperceptions. She would speak of the Lakota traditions, since that is what she knew best. She would usually speak of the three primary principles brought by White Buffalo Calf Maiden, starting with the Lakota word for a child: "wakan yeja." She would then explain that it means "sacred being." She used this as a foundation for discussing a world of values seldom heard by her white audiences as the core of a culture.

This is the background that prepared Pat for her life as a modern day warrior, not fighting with spears or bows and arrows, but with intellect and resourcefulness for Indian education, rights, and the preservation of Indian languages and cultures.

IV

Marriage and Family Life

After graduating from UCLA in 1951 and obtaining her teaching certificate, Pat taught for one year at a school in Long Beach, California. While there, she realized how inadequate traditional curricula were for Indian children. Most of what was taught in school had little to do with generosity, courage, respect, or a true quest for knowledge—all of which are essential Lakota values. The school she worked at celebrated a few secular observances, mainly with superficial treatment. In contrast, certain Lakota ceremonies are considered sacred and essential for what it means to be a human being.

Pat also noticed that traditions and concern about ancestry and progeny were not covered in public schools. In the Lakota way, ancestors for seven generations past are to be remembered and honored, and their stories are to be told. Thoughts should also be concerned with seven generations yet to come. This is considered an essential part of knowing who you are and your heritage. Pat felt new curricula were needed, more suitable for Indian children. This concern would surface later, but now was not the time. Marriage and family were the priorities.

Pat met Charles Edward Locke III (Ned)* while both were attending UCLA. After her year of teaching, the two of them were

---

* He was a descendant of the brother of the famous English philosopher, John Locke.

married and they lived in the Los Angeles area during their first few years of marriage.

Their first child, a girl, lived only about twenty minutes.[18]* Pat had suffered a long and difficult labor with delivery by Cesarean section. Losing the child was hard for her. Her mother stayed with her for six weeks during this trying period, giving Pat comfort and support, stressing the need for her to prepare her body for future wakan yeja (sacred beings or children), telling her she would have another, and then yet another would be given to her. In preparation for future pregnancies, Pat started a rigid diet. It consisted of mainly fresh fruits and vegetables. Two more children were born: Kevin, born in 1954, and Winona (Nona) in 1956. Both pregnancies were difficult and both deliveries were by Cesarean section.

The diet continued through the birth of the two surviving children, and while they were young. She fed them raw fruit, raw milk, yogurt, and brewers' yeast mixed in whatever else she fixed for them.

During these years, Pat's parents lived in Alhambra, California, within about fifteen miles of where the Lockes were living. Sometimes, when the children were young, Pat's parents lived with them. So, as infants, they were often in the arms of their grandparents. When Pat became a public figure, she often stressed the importance of generations living together. To her it is an unequalled source of stability and security.

While the children were young, Pat was not involved in the affairs of the world. She called this period of time in her life "living in a capsule." The full-time attention inside that capsule was devoted to

---

* Shortly after Pat's death, a friend who knew Pat as an adult but had not known about the loss of the first child, called Kevin to tell him of a vivid dream she had of his mother. Pat was in the next world and delighted to be there. There were two children with her. One she knew was Pat's grandson, Hepana, who had been killed in an automobile accident about a year earlier, and the other was a girl about Kevin's age whom she did not recognize. Kevin immediately assumed the woman was witnessing a reunion of his mother with both his nephew and his sister who had lived just twenty minutes.

the children. She would not even let them go to nursery school as she did not want any negative influences to come into their young lives.

Her method of parenting reflected both her Lakota upbringing and her view of the larger world. She was a diligently protective mother, but would never strike or raise her voice to either child. Uppermost in her mind was the consciousness that they were sacred beings, and one cannot strike a sacred being. When the children would drop things or make a mess, especially when Kevin would shove things off his high chair or break things, she would incorporate her knowledge of French, saying: "c'est la vie"—such is life—either out loud or to herself.

Key to her approach for childrearing was that the family must get along. If the children were fighting, fussing, or acting in any way that was unacceptable, she would have them leave the room and tell them to come back when they felt they were ready. They were taught to think of the feelings of others, just as she was taught to do.

Kevin reported that his mother was very gentle and never raised her voice. "In the evenings she would sing and read to us—things that were intellectually stimulating as well as entertaining."[19] There were great family ties and bonding. The result of this method was that as a child, and even as an adult, Kevin would never dream of doing anything that would displease his mother, even slightly. It wasn't out of fear, but out of deep respect.

When the children were young, Pat became close friends with Frances Makepeace, who shared her love of family and children. Frances did not drive and they became acquainted when Pat gave her a ride one day. Both had small children and the two families enjoyed many outings together, especially going to the Balboa and Manhattan beaches. The children would splash about and Pat loved to body surf. At night they would all go to the beach and have bonfire parties—a practice that is no longer legal.

Frances contracted polio and had a long convalescence in the hospital. Pat was a frequent visitor, and when Frances got out of the hospital the families continued their treks to the beach. There were

101 steps down to the beach and Ned wanted to carry Frances, but Pat would not let anyone else carry her. She insisted that she would do it. So, hoisting Frances on her back, piggyback style, she carried her down to the beach, and when they were ready to leave, Pat carried her back up the 101 steps. In an understatement, Frances said, "She was a very strong woman, but also petite. Looking at her you would never realize how strong she was."[20]

While living in the Los Angeles area, Ned was working as a furnace installer. Then he got a position with the Systems Development Corporation doing contract work for the military. This was during the Cold War, and the United States government set up the Distance Early Warning System (DEW Line) with radar installations throughout the northern hemisphere, from Alaska through the northern tier of states into Greenland. Those radar installations, together with constant jet fighter surveillance flights, were designed to give advanced warning of an expected airstrike from the Soviet Union.

This meant the family moved often. The first move was to Great Falls, Montana in about 1959 where Ned worked at the Malmstrom Air Force Base. They lived out of town a little ways where there was a wonderful hill for sliding in the winter. There was also a well-used skating pond nearby. During summers, weekends were spent camping and having picnics. And there were always dogs—Pat loved dogs and usually had several around. Kevin was the only non-white kid in the class and was picked on a great deal because of being Indian, but he never told his mom. He just accepted that as normal.

After two years in Great Falls, Ned was transferred back to L.A. Kevin still remembers the address where they lived—19543 Bowers Drive. His mom made him memorize the address in case he got lost. That seems like a lesson learned from Pat's Chicago experience in which she was lost, but knew the name of the hotel. While in Los Angeles, Pat started her graduate studies by taking courses at UCLA in Public Administration. But, in 1966 Ned was assigned to Elmendorf Air Force Base, just outside of Anchorage, Alaska, so the family moved again.

Wherever she was, Pat did some work to supplement the family income, but only on her terms. She would work as long as she was not separated from her children. In Los Angeles, Great Falls, and Anchorage she gave classes, usually at a local YMCA or YWCA. Her instructions covered a range of activities, including swimming, tennis, guitar, exercise, and dancing lessons—ballet, interpretive, ethnic, and ballroom. Whenever she had a class, Kevin and Nona would always be with her. When she taught swimming she would have the youngsters in life jackets or inner tubes, and they would float about and splash around while their mother was giving lessons.

During guitar and dancing lessons the children were also close at hand. Nona recalled how, as a little girl, she loved the dancing classes. There would be fifteen to twenty people in the house and Nona took great delight in watching the people swirling around. When it was time for tennis lessons, young Kevin would run hither and yon, shagging tennis balls that had gone astray. Pat, like her father, was a great tennis player and loved to play. She was also a beautiful woman and a real knockout when dressed for tennis. Men would come around to ogle her beautiful legs. Nona recalled that when she was a teenager her mother said: "Oh, my legs cause great problems."[21]

Ned had to travel a great deal because of his work, and that caused a lot of strain in the marriage. But in spite of the marital difficulties, Pat was not one to belittle him. Instead, she recalled that he was a very good father to Nona and Kevin, and was very loving and attentive with them. Pat said that in several places where they lived there were prejudicial experiences that were hard for the children to cope with, but she was able to act as a buffer because she was not working full-time and Ned was consistently protective and supportive.

The family's move to Alaska in 1966 proved to be a major turning point in Pat's life.

V

Alaska

Life was turbulent for Pat when the family moved to Anchorage. Her marriage was in jeopardy and attempts to salvage it were not working. The marriage ended while the family was there. Kevin reported that the tension and bickering at home were so stressful that it was a relief for him when his parents separated.

Despite her own problems, Pat was alert to the needs of others. She saw that the Natives moving to Anchorage from the villages were facing special challenges while trying to adjust to the city. Life was confusing for many of them and they did not have the skills needed to cope. A major difference was in how they viewed the world. Pat saw the societal contradiction that the Natives were trying to make sense of. She thought action was needed to help people with different worldviews live in a community foreign to them.

In 1967 Pat started the Anchorage Welcome Center for Indians, Eskimos, and Aleuts who had moved to Anchorage from the villages. Many of them did not speak English and found the city a hard place to live. The purpose of the center was to help people find jobs and housing and, in general, cope with city life. It was Pat's first full-time work outside the home.

Pat was sensitive to the basic differences between urban and village thinking. She could see clearly through the eyes of both villagers and urban people; was aware of the inevitable problems that arose because of misunderstandings; and could help both groups understand, accept, and even appreciate the views of the others. And she had a talent for communicating her insights.

There was an excellent example of this difference during the time that Pat was running the welcome center. The Anchorage post office had been opened twenty-four hours a day so box holders doing shift work could get their mail any time. Because it was always open, it became an attractive place for homeless people. Seeing these people sleeping on the post office floor was offensive for many Anchorage residents. Pressure was brought to bear on the postal authorities to close the facility so the homeless could not get in. The policy was changed and the doors were locked at night. That was the end of the problem and a relief as far as many people of Anchorage were concerned—a reflection of the value system of urban America, where there is a preoccupation with economic well-being and personal comfort.

In contrast to that, in most villages there is an unspoken concern about the well-being of everyone. Therefore, it was seen differently through the eyes of villagers who were new to Anchorage: the welfare of others was more important than being tidy. Three young Eskimo men from different villages, who spent a lot of time at the welcome center, were discussing this and their thoughts reflected village thinking. They raised the question: "Where are they (the homeless) supposed to go?" That was the important question for them, and undoubtedly they discussed the situation with Pat. While it is not clear what her role was in this discussion, if she was involved, her insight was no doubt invaluable. She would have used her brilliance in being able to see both sides of issues and explaining the thinking of one group to the other in a manner that was nonjudgmental and promoted understanding and calm.

She felt a friendly place was needed where village people could find help, understanding, and companionship. Together with a few other people, she found a suitable place in the heart of downtown Anchorage, close to the present-day Captain Cook Hotel. While it wasn't a homeless shelter, she was able to use it to provide one warm meal, five days-a-week, and give village people a gathering place.

Beyond this she was able to arrange for some of the Natives to get some basic resources. She persuaded local dentists to help the Natives from the villages who had lost their teeth and had no money. She also started camps for Native children. She was even arrested on one occasion for taking part in a peaceful demonstration for Native rights.[22]

Maynard Eaken, an Inuit Eskimo from Kotzebue, recalls coming to Anchorage as a young man. A friend took him to the center, and, as a recovering alcoholic, he thought it was a good place to start an AA group. What he found was something even greater. It was a place to hang out, meet friends, and find out what was going on in the community. Years later, he recalled the warmth and concern Pat radiated. He said she was always busy helping someone find housing, a job, filling out forms, or whatever was needed.[23] When Maynard was asked about her being arrested for a peaceful protest he said he didn't know anything about it, but it wouldn't surprise him. He said she would always stand up against injustice and wasn't afraid to speak her mind no matter what the consequences might be.

For Maynard and countless other villagers, the center was a valuable asset in the challenge of adjusting to life in Anchorage. He knew she was operating on a shoestring budget, but somehow managed to make things work and served simple, regular meals by scrounging here and there. Maynard also recalled that Pat's teenage children— Kevin and Winona—were nearly always there. Even though the center played a vital role in helping villagers in their adjustment to Anchorage, it was not sustained after Pat left.

The welcome center was her Rubicon. Like a butterfly emerging from its cocoon, she irreversibly left her self-imposed "capsule" and started her life of activism. She began to hone her networking skills, became comfortable working with people of all strata, and could see all aspects of many different social issues. This talent was an important factor in the success of the welcome center, as well as the many challenges she faced later in life.

The years in Alaska were difficult for Pat, and a key person, Art Davidson, showed up at just the right time.[24] When asked about Pat, Art told of their first meeting: "On a summer day I needed some help clearing some trees and I heard about a welcome center that had been set up by this Lakota woman to help people who had come in from the bush to adjust to being in Anchorage. I went in there and asked this woman if she knew of anyone who could help for a day or two. She said she did not know anyone and I said I would call her back in a few days. She said she didn't have a phone because she was just moving and didn't know where she was going. I said, 'OK, I'll check back in a few days,' so I went about my life. I was also looking for a place to live with my wife, Mossy, and one infant son and one on the way."[25]

Art found a large A-frame duplex in the woods behind Anchorage. Both apartments were empty and he told Mossy about the woman he had met who was also looking for a place to live. He suggested letting her know about the other apartment. Mossy agreed. The next day he went back to the center and said, "Hi, I don't know if you remember me. My name is Art." She said she remembered and that she still hadn't found anyone to help.

Art said that was all right and mentioned that he had found a place for his family. It was a duplex and both apartments were empty. He asked if she might be interested in the other apartment. She said she would look into it. The next evening she showed up with her two children and wrapped-up gifts. She said, "We brought you a gift—it's our custom—when we come to visit we bring a gift."

After looking around the place, she told Art, "You know, we would like to share this house with you." So, she and her two children moved in.

Over time Art realized that she was also looking for friendship. It was a vulnerable time for her. Her marriage was ending and she had two teenage children. They were moving from the marital home out on their own and she was concerned about finding a safe place for her and her children to live.

When you are alone with teenage children, there are many concerns: Will they be safe? What will their peers be like? What kind of friends will they make? She had so many challenges: being a good mother; trying to get her bearings after her marriage ended; she had to earn her own living; and she wanted a good life for her children—for them to get a good education and be around good people.

As Art and Pat became close friends, the two households became one, like an extended family. When there were tense moments with the children, Art was able to help and a strong bond was created. While they may not have been related through family lines or a business connection, there was a strong attachment that persisted over the years.

Soon after the Lockes moved into the adjoining apartment, Mossy went into labor. With a twinkle in his eye, Art explained, "Pat rushed

Pat addressing a group in Anchorage, Alaska

her to the hospital and she loved it! She ran the red lights and she was ready to tell the police, 'I'm rushing this woman to the hospital and you'd better get out of my way or go ahead of me with your flashing red lights.' It was her sense of defiance for a good cause. She had reason to defy the rules and authority and they couldn't do anything about it because she was taking this lady to the hospital."

This was also a time when Alaska was going through the cycle of history that had played out decades earlier in the rest of the United States. The territory was on the verge of becoming a state, and the state would get its own land. Many evenings and weekends, Native Alaskan leaders would come to see Pat. They would talk about what they could do to help the people in the villages. These leaders— many of them quite young—asked for advice about how to retain their languages and get better medical care, and they discussed issues concerning pending land claims.

It was the time for a new kind of Indian war, not on the battlefield but with public hearings. Pat, and others like her, would speak about the rights people have that should be honored. While she would speak with conviction and deep feeling, she also did her homework and would cite the facts. She would point out that rights of the Native people were written into the purchase agreement with Russia. Article III of the "Treaty with Russia" dated March 30, 1867 clearly states that the aborigines of Alaska shall enjoy all the rights and protection of the law available within the rest of the United States. Those rights spelled out in the purchase agreement were to be respected. She would go to hearings and meet with whatever officials she could. Wherever she went, she was armed with more than emotion and righteous indignation. She had her facts in order.

She also inspired others to speak out. In that way she was like a grandmother or an aunt. Her role was to build confidence so the Natives could step forward and have the courage to fight for what was right. She told them not to worry if they didn't have all the big words. They could stand before a Congressional committee or a governor or a mayor and say, "Look, these people have rights."

In her many-faceted way, Pat was an influential factor working for Native rights in Alaska. At the same time, this process helped her to develop her own skills of encouraging others and finding people who could bring about change. She didn't hold important political or corporate positions. In her quiet and unobtrusive way she encouraged, nurtured, and strategized with many young Alaskan Natives who were to become future leaders of the community. Harold Napoleon, an Eskimo leader from Hooper Bay, recalled that as a young man he and many other young Native leaders would gather at Pat's home and discuss important Native issues. Pat's role was to provide hospitality and encouragement. She would give advice only when asked.[26]

Art said she would often talk to him about a wide range of issues. She would say how important the traditions, language, and customs were for young people and would lament the fact that many of these things are slipping away. She said, "We can't live in the past. We have to let the wisdom of the past, our medicine men, and our ancestors guide us and give us direction. We also have to have the means to cope with this modern world."

Her hope was that her children would be capable, both in their hearts and their souls, to live in both worlds. While retaining the Lakota values of wisdom, courage, respect, and generosity, they needed skills to deal with people in different situations in the wider world.

For her, those days in Alaska were a springboard. She was transitioning from being a full-time mother caring for her children to an activist speaking out for Native and indigenous people. She was finding her voice and encouraging others to raise their voices for justice, for fairness, and for a way of life that made sense. She stressed the idea that youth should be inspired to uphold the preservation of Native rights and spiritual values while also being given the opportunity to get a good education.

She went from being a mother to her children to the wider field of being a devoted mother, aunt, sister, and grandmother to many. She became known as *Unchi* (Uŋčí—pronounced ung-chee, which means *grandmother*). From this springboard in Alaska she became active in aboriginal affairs throughout the world, encouraging leaders to stand up and fight for their rights.

In order to support her family, she continued to teach swimming lessons at the YMCA, as well as guitar and dancing lessons. She also taught at the Alaska Methodist University (now Alaska Pacific University) during the summer of 1970, which turned out to be the first of eight colleges where she taught.

She had an amazing range of friends. They included the poorest of people with no education, people who lived in little houses and shacks out on Reservations, and people who struggled in cities; and also some of the most well-known writers, intellectuals, visionaries, and politicians of her time. She could converse and communicate so clearly with them all. She spoke in a direct and heartfelt way with anyone. That was part of her beauty.

Art was asked how he thought she became the person she turned out to be. He replied, "Well, I tend to believe that it's both by nature and by nurturing. You have to realize that Pat came from an incredibly strong evolutionary gene pool of people who were great, great survivors from both sides of her family—two different tremendous, terrific, very strong Native American cultures. She had grandmothers and grandfathers and ancestors all the way back who were incredibly strong as warriors, as hunters, as providers, but also as communicators.

"I think that without a doubt, Pat Locke was a very intelligent woman and she came by a Native intelligence, from her Native heritage. It's not just an intelligence that can help you add and subtract, but it's an intelligence that observes carefully, is able to use wisdom—which is often in short supply today, and also it's always tempered by a caring for others, other people, other creatures, and for the Earth.

"Communicating, and being able to make peace, to cooperate and work with other people who may at some times be your enemy—these are things that run very deep in her people and you have to realize it was not an easy life for Indians here in North America. Their life may be beautiful in some ways, but it can't be over-romanticized. And her ancestors were very, very strong in many, many ways. I'm sure that the brilliance of these people, whose names have never been recorded in a book or a graduation of university, are as bright as the Einsteins and the Newtons and any of the great statesmen of today."

He went on to say that she shared with him the Lakota concept of "mitakuye oyasin"—that we're all related. Modern biologists say the same thing from a different perspective. We are related to the two-legged, the four-legged, the little rodents, the winged ones, those with fins, and all creatures of a common mother—the Earth. We share so much DNA. We share much in this evolutionary journey. Art explained, ". . . there was great respect that came down from her ancestors for this Earth, for the buffalo that they hunted, for the deer that they hunted, for the fish they took. There is a respect, even a reverence, for the game that provides sustenance—food, clothing, shelter, and tools. This is an understanding that is not commonly found in the modern world. It is different from herding cattle and sheep and keeping pigs pinned up and then slaughtering them and then wrapping them up in neat little packages at the grocery store with scant thought of the interrelatedness and interconnectedness of all creatures."

"She was also a product of the difficult times her people had to go through: the terrible suffering, persecution, execution of her family members, by this government—ordered by a president who is so revered by many, Abraham Lincoln. In his relations with the Indians his policies were brutal. Indians were considered as an enemy to exterminate because they were in the way of the Western settlement. She encouraged Native Americans to stand up and say, 'Look, we're here. We're still here.'

"So, Pat was a warrior: not fighting with spears and arrows and Winchester rifles from the backs of horses with cavalry wagons and swords. She was a fierce, fierce warrior who fought for her people and she fought in many other ways. She fought by setting up colleges—she was forever going to Washington, D.C. to lobby. She fought by encouraging and promoting young people to become leaders, to believe in themselves, believe in what they can do, believe in their vision of justice, of the kind of life they want for their children and their grandchildren."

Art was of the opinion that "Pat became who she was not only from her distant ancestors, but also from recent generations of struggle and fight and strife that her people and her family went through. . . . Her parents made sure that she got a good education. . . . And she's a very good writer, a very good editor, and how she applied herself when she went to college, how she learned every single day, talking to people, reading, observing, listening. She became an incredible larger-than-life person. I don't want to say a larger-than-life woman because that would be limiting. She became one of the great, great souls and great people of her time, period!"

Art went on to say, "I don't think of her as a Native American leader, per se. I don't think of her just as a woman's leader. I just think of her as one of the great people of this century, of our times. And it was a great, great lesson to me. I benefited in many, many ways from my relationship with her."

Over the years they would see each other off and on. Sometimes there would be months or even a year or two between visits, but their paths would cross again. And there was always a deep, deep bond between them.

Art continued, "Years later I was looking for a book that could show me how Native people around the world were struggling. It struck me that many people, many enlightened people, caring people, were concerned about endangered species—about the rhinoceros, about the tigers, the Siberian tigers, about different species of fish and butterflies and frogs and birds, many of which are in danger. But then we don't think about how whole cultures, how whole peoples, who have their cultural ways that evolved over thousands and thousands of years, that they too can be endangered, that their languages can disappear, that the people dwindle down to a precious few, and then disappear. And so I looked in all the big bookstores and every catalog I could find. And I found books about the . . . Aborigines or about the Apaches, or about the Ainu in Japan. But I couldn't find a book that showed me the phenomenon going around the whole world, where maybe even indigenous cultures are threatened, they're being put to the brink, which shows me what they're struggling with.

"So, I went to Pat and I said, 'I think there's an important book, to bring the voices of these people in South America, tribal people in Africa, in Asia, Australia, New Zealand, North America, Russia, and even Europe.' And she encouraged me, she said, 'This is an important thing to do; I'll help you in every way I can.' And so she became a great mentor to me, she had always been a mentor, but she became specifically a mentor to me in going about gathering, meeting the people, and giving voice to what they were struggling with. So she was a terrific help with that and was with me all the way, whether introducing me to people, giving me the encouragement, giving me advice. And later, as I was writing and telling the story, she would read it and she would give me her thoughts."

Pat was involved with every phase of Art's book, *Endangered Peoples,** for which Rigoberta Menchú† wrote the foreword. Art confided that if it were not for Pat, the book would not have been written.

He said, "People like Rigoberta Menchú and Pat Locke were really inspiring leaders of their age, working in different ways. And so we were very, very happy to have that book come out, published in different languages. It is not an anthropological book, but it's just a forum, a way to let this speak. Leaders of many different tribal groups talk about how they're faced with problems about hydroelectric dams or the forest being cut in Sarawak or the treaty of the Maoris being turned against them or the Aborigines of Australia just with no treaty rights whatsoever, just being marginalized and persecuted and often

---

* This richly illustrated 195 page, 9x12, coffee table book has beautiful pictures of people from all over the world. They are shown doing the ordinary things that have been a vital part of their cultures for centuries. The book demonstrates how the encroachment of western civilization is endangering the way of life of countless people throughout the world.

† Rigoberta Menchú was from Guatemala. Her family was persecuted because of their political activism on behalf of indigenous rights. Both of her parents were assassinated by the government because they spoke out for education, healthcare, and land rights. Rigoberta wrote letters and had petitions circulated. She was forced to live underground because she was hunted by authorities. In 1998 she was awarded both the Nobel Peace Prize and the Prince of Asturias Award.

infected with diseases and sent away from their homes for education. Pat was a great inspiration for this type of work, and I know that she worked with others in many, many different initiatives."

Later, Art reflected, "I've been very blessed, very blessed to have been—to have known Pat, and to be close to her and to be inspired by her, and to know through her life, how one person can influence so many, often in quiet ways. Not as an official head of some corporation or committee or organization, but just person-to-person, through her wisdom, through courage, her unselfish sharing of her time with others who were also working for justice for people.

"That's the way it went. From meeting Pat Locke while looking for a couple of people to help me clear some underbrush, to being a housemate with her family and my family as our families became one, to really feeling that she was sometimes like a sister, sometimes like a mother, sometimes like an aunt, and of course, in her later years, we all called her Unchi."

Art planted a bristle cone pine tree on his property that he calls "Unchi." The bristle cone pine is thought to live longer than any other known single, living organism—up to 5,000 years. That tree is a fitting memorial for one whose legacy will live on, destined to be there for generations yet unborn. Whenever the tree comes into view, Art thinks of Pat and inspiration is renewed.

While Pat was still in Alaska, a position became available in Colorado with the Western Interstate Counsel on Higher Education, known as WICHE. This is a regional organization created by the Western Regional Education Compact, adopted in the 1950s by Western states. It started operations in 1953 and moved to Boulder, Colorado in 1955. They were setting up community colleges throughout the west to serve people better. It was apparent that the existing universities and colleges were not meeting the needs of many rural people, including Native Americans. Their program included finding Native Americans to help set up colleges. Pat went to Colorado for an interview and surprised them with her candor.

During the interview mention was made of the holidays she would have off. Her response was, "We would have Columbus Day off? Why would I want to celebrate Columbus Day? Do you think it is something for Native Americans to celebrate? In your eyes, we were discovered by Europeans, but look at all the trouble that came to us later! The Fourth of July? Well, I'm patriotic to our country, but you know there are many other holidays and many other things that our people observe: the coming of spring, various rights and ceremonies in the summer time when the moon is full, the harvest ceremony, the fall ceremony, things we do in winter. You have to understand that if you hire me, you are hiring someone who respects the traditions of my people, and not just my people—the Lakota and my ancestors—but other Native Americans. Any work we do in education is going to have to be done from that point of view and I don't just mean different holidays, but different ways of looking at the world and looking at our lives and where we are and where we come from and where we want to go." She said what was in her heart, not just what she thought a prospective employer might like to hear. She got the position and the family moved to Boulder, Colorado.

She did not forget Alaska. Soon after she was hired she returned to Alaska in an official capacity for WICHE. A picture in the *All-Alaska Weekly*, dated August 13, 1971, shows Pat and other WICHE officials in Alaska meeting with prominent political and educational leaders.

In order for Kevin to have a strong male model and mentor, she arranged for him to return to Alaska during the summer of 1971 to help Art build his house. More importantly, she wanted Kevin to learn from Art about his work on conservation issues. She wanted Kevin to have the experience of helping the Native people. Kevin returned to Alaska to work with Art, who became like an uncle to him. Both have reported that it was a wonderful summer that developed an enduring relationship.

VI

Tribal Colleges

Pat's work at the Western Interstate Council on Higher Education (WICHE) was the beginning of her most aggressive activism. Her task was to encourage colleges in rural areas and among minorities, but her sights went beyond colleges. She was interested in all aspects of Indians gaining self-determination. She felt that education was important, both for its own sake and as a tool for her broader agenda. She had a vision of a world in which Indian people could control their own destiny. One in which they could function in the white man's world and still retain their heritage, their values, and their language. Tribal colleges were an important aspect of Indian empowerment.

About the time that Pat started working for WICHE, Douglas Skye—a relative of hers—was elected chairman of the tribal council on the Standing Rock Reservation. According to Duane Claymore, who was on the Council at that time, it was in the late 1960s when Pat gave Douglas the idea that he should start a college on the Reservation. Douglas agreed that this was a good idea. His first step was to ask Pat to write a proposal for a college, which she did.

Douglas was a recovering alcoholic and a strong advocate of AA. He had gotten to know a lot of people throughout South Dakota because of his work with AA. This included Senator Karl Mundt. Although no longer in the U.S. Senate, Mundt knew many important people, was sympathetic to the idea of tribal colleges, and helped push the idea forward. Douglas died of a heart attack shortly after the process was started and the vice-chairman, Melvin White Eagle, took over and carried it out. Pat's role was giving Douglas the idea and writing the proposal. Others saw it through to completion.

The college, originally called Standing Rock College, received funding and was established in Ft. Yates, North Dakota. A ceremony honoring those responsible for the college made no mention of the work that either Douglas or Pat had done at the beginning. This disappointed many who knew the full story.[27]

If the lack of recognition bothered Pat, she never mentioned it. She was more interested in results than credit and had already moved on to other things. But the experience of writing the proposal for the establishment of the college whet her appetite, helped sharpen her writing skills, demonstrated the power of networking, and launched her on her crusade on behalf of Indian education.

She reasoned that tribes needed to have control of their own schools. This would involve a multistep process. She said that in order for the schools to control the curricula, they should be able to make choices; in order to make choices, they had to have sovereign rights; in order to have sovereign rights, there must be recognition by the government and less management from the variable advantages and disadvantages of patronage from the Bureau of Indian Affairs (BIA); in order for that to happen, enabling legislation was needed; and in order to get enabling legislation, it was necessary for legislators to take up the battle. She needed to find legislators who would champion her cause. The challenge was great, her vision was clear, her resolve strong, and she was on her way.

In working for tribal colleges, there were a myriad of questions that had to be faced. Why is it important to have colleges on the Reservations? Why can't Indian youth travel to established schools elsewhere? Can they get a quality education at small schools on Reservations? This last question is part of the general criticism that smaller schools, including community colleges and private schools, are less rigorous and therefore inferior.

Pat dismissed such criticism and saw much more to education than simply sitting in a classroom and gaining book-learning. She had started from a community college and realized that while formal schooling can be an important part of, and springboard for, education, it was but an entry point for learning. Instead, she looked to some more basic and fundamental purposes to explain the importance of having tribal colleges.

In the Western world formal education is often thought of as a way to gain personal, material advantage through vocational, professional, or other training. Statistics are cited showing that college graduates earn more money than nongraduates. Where is that advantage more vital than on Reservations, where poverty is such an overwhelming problem?

People in some parts of the world do not see formal education for personal gain, but as a means for the younger generation to better serve their country and their people. This view is consistent with the Lakota value that the good of the group takes priority over the good of the individual.

A more philosophical view is that the purpose of formal education is to perpetuate a culture and groom responsible citizens. That need is strongly felt in most American Indian communities. Historically, from their Latin foundation, the purpose of schools was to produce well-rounded, productive members of society. A broad range of knowledge and understanding was considered more important than specific skills. Again, tribal colleges uniquely prepare graduates to appreciate and contribute to their communities and the world because, in addition to standard academic education, there is an emphasis on understanding their ancestral roots and cultural traditions.

Pat understood other concerns as well. It can be frightening and intimidating for someone from the Reservation to go to the unfamiliar surroundings of a different culture, which all too often involves racial harassment. Ties to the extended families on the Reservation are powerful, attractive, and comforting forces. Youth often feel a responsibility for the care of a parent, sibling, grandparent, or other relative. Choices have to be made between leaving the Reservation to get an education and neglecting a strongly felt duty. Duty usually wins. Finally, the full appreciation of knowledge, skills, and respect for cultural roots grows best at home.

Pat knew the challenge. She, as well as a few others, had a dream. Even though their dreams were slightly different, all were struggling diligently to bring higher education to the Reservations. The differences, however, caused serious problems. They would often stumble over each other and seemingly work at crosspurposes in their common and monumental quest to empower Native Americans.

By 1972 there were six Indian colleges in the United States, located in Rosebud and Pine Ridge in South Dakota; Belcourt and Fort Yates in North Dakota; Tsaile, Arizona; and Davis, California. They faced common problems: geographic and cultural isolation; majority Indian administrators, often inexperienced in higher education administration; small student bodies; chronically unpredictable funding; and students from the lowest economic areas of the country.[28] The school leaders, together with Pat from WICHE and a representative from the U.S. Department of Education, formed the American Indian Higher Education Consortium (AIHEC) to help deal with these issues.

From the outset there were both internal and external problems. Externally, there was constant discouragement from federal agencies. Internally, there was a conflict of objectives between AIHEC and WICHE. AIHEC was focused on getting charter colleges on Reservations. Pat and WICHE had a broader agenda. They felt tribes should have options for education and that language preservation and sovereignty issues were vital parts of the mix. AIHEC saw these as side issues that blurred, sabotaged, and could ultimately defeat their primary goal of charter colleges.

In addition to differing objectives there was an immediate and practical dispute over money. The BIA had grants. Both organizations were after the same funds. The rift broadened and deepened. The AIHEC board and Pat, on behalf of WICHE, tenaciously held to conflicting views. Other differences added to the problem and led to long-term animosity between the consortium and Pat.

Yet, they had to work with Congress, which prefers working with one leader on a single proposal. Instead, it was a fractious group with internal squabbling, trying to accomplish the impossible. It was like squeezing two different colored marshmallows through the eye of a single needle.

Originally, there were no champions in Congress. The group would march from hall to hall and door to door to find people who would promote the needed legislation. How did Pat go about getting Congressional cooperation? She had a genius for knowing who was approachable, who had the capacity to understand the issues, and who had the power to achieve her goals. She also had a talent, not only for finding people who could do what needed to be done, but to get them to put their energies to work for her objectives.

Harlene Green, who worked with her at a later time on language preservation, explained that her technique was to find someone who knew a particular Congressman and had access to him. Together with three or four of his constituents—usually women—they would get an appointment. Pat would stride up to the Congressman while the women of her entourage would stand silently, stoically staring at the Congressman with their arms folded across their chests. Pat would say, "This is what you are going to do. . . ." Then she would outline the strategy he was to follow. She did not argue. She did not harangue. She just told him what was expected with no threats, implied or otherwise. She made it clear what his role was to be. The presence of the women, silent and determined, made the desired impression.

Harlene said they must have looked like a bunch of Geronimos. The poor Congressman would sit there, facing a group of resolute, determined, and unflinching Geronimos. He usually did as he was told. She said, "The first time we did that it frightened me. Most of us would just walk in. All we had to do was just stand there."[29]

Dr. Janine Pease-Windy Boy, former AIHEC member and tribal college president, wrote her doctoral thesis on the development of tribal colleges. She said, "It was just so amazing that they were able to do this—brilliant, geniuses really, brilliant, brilliant work. It was marvelous to see, I mean, I am so awestruck, I am just awestruck. It was the pinnacle of legislative success from people who amounted to nothing. They had no clout. They had no giant voter block behind them. They had no set of Congressmen or Senators in their hip pocket. Nobody cared about them. So they had to be driven by the weight and the importance of the issues."[30]

The group found endless setbacks, but they did not get discouraged. If someone in authority said *no,* they were just spurred on. Being rebuffed served as an inspiration to go one step further or use a different approach. David Gipp, a former director of the consortium, recalled, "if we had listened and accepted (the advice of the government officials), we would have been beaten."[31] Instead, there was always more work and research to be done, led by Pat.

An example of the challenge was seen when they went to the Carter White House to meet with someone who was supposed to be the expert with whom they should work. He was asked, "Why are you working with the tribal colleges? How do you come to be working with Indians?" His response was: "I was assigned to work with homosexuals, Indians, and Jews." He had no background, let alone expertise, in matters involving Indians. He had never even met an Indian before—not even one—and he had no appreciation of what was to be accomplished or what he was expected to do. This was the level of "expert" assistance they got.

Pease described the irony of the two-edged challenge. She said, "Dealing with that level of understanding in the government, and then to bash at each other over these really difficult fundamental principles of sovereignty, education, and distribution of funds and all of that. . . . Then to try to get support from people like that made it a most difficult challenge."

There were many hearings, and long position papers needed to be written. Pease went on to say, "And Pat would know best, without a doubt. People in Congress read the correspondence from both sides. There were some phenomenal people in the committees. When I was doing my research,* many of the people from the

---

* For her EdD thesis, written several years after these episodes.

committees were still there. It was impressive to see what a long-lasting impact it had made."

Among members of Congress there was a strong and justifiable fear that allowing colleges on Reservations would lead to more contentious and potentially explosive sovereignty issues that could destroy them politically. None of them were eager to face questions about fishing and territorial rights and a host of other matters. Many otherwise sympathetic Congressmen backed off from their support of tribal colleges out of a realistic fear of these potentially hazardous issues, especially fishing rights. Because of all these other problems involving Native land and other rights, establishing colleges on the Reservations was seen as but an entry into very difficult areas politically. It was complicated.

American Indian policy is complex and confusing. The result of more than a century of broken promises and conflicting legislation and regulations created an often contradictory pool of procedures and rules in which these beleaguered champions of Indian education had to swim.

After the Tribally Controlled Community College Assistance Act of 1978 was passed, AIHEC decided changes were needed. This is not unusual as amendments are frequently used to correct some unforeseen problem in original legislation. There were three paragraphs that members of AIHEC felt should be rewritten.

Pat, and therefore WICHE, had nothing but antipathy for those changes. They testified about it before Congress and managed to acquire a strong alliance, including the Indian Education Association, of which Pat was vicepresident. These were hard times that strained relations even more.

Pease conceded, "She was indeed a scholar. There were scholars of tremendous proportion on both sides of this dialogue. They didn't go about their conflict with fisticuffs. They didn't bash each other in the mouth; they didn't yell and scream bad names or bad words. They wrote about these issues; they were deeply issue-driven. And they analyzed.

"The prospect for these tribal colleges was like standing on a house of cards and all the cards under you are falling away. In the meantime, here was Pat, arguing over sovereignty. All the tribal colleges were having bake sales to stay alive. They were meeting in ratty places. Here comes Pat with a budget and money from WICHE and she was able to stay in nice places."

The internal confrontations also started the final break between the organizations. Pease reported that, "It wasn't long before AIHEC filed for divorce from Mrs. Locke."

The rancor over these differences was so strong and enduring among members of AIHEC that when Pease was collecting material for her thesis, one former AIHEC member refused to be interviewed when he learned that she had interviewed Pat. Pease said, "If you want to know, the members of the tribal colleges think that except for Pat Locke the legislation would have passed much faster. I don't subscribe to that. I do know that since I became a president of a tribal college and worked through all of these issues, she uncovered issues we had to face and that later were of benefit—including unforeseen questions that would affect accreditation." Pease reported that most members of AIHEC dismissed the differences as a personality clash. However, she felt that Pat held a deeply seated, but different and broader vision.

Gary Kimble, who had worked with Pat on sacred site preservation, shared his view of the situation. He felt that much of the criticism was because of jealousy when Pat was awarded the MacArthur Fellowship grant. He said she was the one who took the lead, ". . . this is something they don't give her credit for, but all her friends know this. She put the framework together that started funding for the colleges.

"Even though the higher-ups in AIHEC don't give her credit, those of us who have enough memory and were around know that Pat put it together and got the legislation passed and [got] funding from the federal government."[32]

The younger generation of Indian educators, who were not part of the early struggles, see things differently. Wayne Stein, who was President of the Sitting Bull (nee Standing Rock) college and AIHEC, expressed the greatest respect for Pat Locke and the work she did. The antipathy had vanished from the organization.[33]

Pat's greater range of concerns was apparent years later when Pease interviewed her for her research. "When I interviewed her, she would talk about other things more than tribal colleges. Pat had a much larger agenda than those of us who were involved primarily with tribal education. I'd ask her a question about getting support for the colleges and she would wander over to other things such as discrimination, laws, and other issues."

Pease said of Pat: "In the annals of history, I think Pat Locke will be most remembered for Indian education and the self-determination act. They had set up a section of self-determination that allowed communities to have tribal schools. In the two years following passage of the Act, they cleaned it up a bit and she was very instrumental in providing for the tribal control elements of that law. She was involved in about fifteen tribes. . . . She had become quite a leader in Indian higher education."*

Getting the legislation was just part of the need. There was a major problem of getting tribal leaders to understand the importance of education and have control of the schools. Pat traveled extensively to meet with tribal councils, pointing out the importance of preserving their language and their cultures and having control of the curricula for their schools. It was vital to systematically bring the culture into the consciousness of the next generation. Otherwise the wisdom and ways of the Indian cultures would vanish from the earth.

Years later, Pease became involved with Native Hawaiian and Maori language specialists. When Pat learned that she was involved

---

* While she worked with many other tribes, the ones listed on her resume were, "Assistance to Northern Ute, Pasqua Yaqui, Tohono O'Odham, Menominee Nation, Red Lake Nation, Cherokee Nation of Oklahoma, Standing Rock Sioux Nation, Sisseton-Wahpeton Sioux Tribe, Oneida Nation, Mile Lacs Band of Chippewa, Blackfeet Nation, and Mandan / Hidatsa / Arikara Affiliated Tribes of North Dakota, in the development of tribal education codes, language policy and education departments." Ron Walters, Director of Resource Development at the Sitting Bull College, identified thirty tribes in which her efforts contributed to, "Education departments and tribal education codes."

with language issues, their relationship changed from antagonists and their friendship ripened. They would talk of a whole different realm and would make a point to see each other and discuss language preservation.[34]

Results

What has been the result of these efforts to promote tribal colleges? Tom Aman, Chairman of the Capital Campaign, reported in 2006 that the Sitting Bull College alone graduates about forty Native Americans each year. That is twice the number of Indian students who graduated from all the South Dakota state colleges combined. All together, those schools graduate only about twenty Indian students per year.[35]

A consistent theme of those who have gone through the tribal colleges is their desire—no, their passion—to give back to their home communities, their Reservation, and their tribe.

Ron His Horse is Thunder, a descendant of Sitting Bull, is a good example. He started his college education as one of the early students at Sitting Bull College. From there he transferred to Black Hills State University. He earned his Juris doctorate (law degree) in 1988 from the University of South Dakota. He worked as a lawyer in the private sector for a time before giving up a promising and potentially lucrative career by turning his attention to education for his people.[36] For eleven years he was President of the Sitting Bull College and is now the Tribal Chairman of the Standing Rock Reservation.

Laurel Vermillion, PhD, was the President of the Sitting Bull College in 2009. She was one of the first students in 1973. This meant driving seventy-five miles each way on a gravel road twice a week. She said, ". . . we would meet with Dr. Jack Barden, who was our instructor. We didn't have a room, so we would follow him around with our tablets and our pencils until we could find a place to sit down in a hallway or corner; we would put chairs together in a circle."[37]

That was the beginning. In recent years enrollment at Sitting Bull has remained above 250 students.* The 2006–2008 catalog has a full range of science, math, English, humanities, business, and criminal justice courses, as well as many trade programs. It lists eight certificate courses, nineteen two-year programs, and offers both Bachelor of Science and Bachelor of Arts degrees.

Dr. Vermillion uses her own experience to encourage students who get discouraged and want to give up. When she came back to the college as an administrator she felt that she had come full circle. She said, "If it hadn't been for the college (on the Reservation), I never would have gone to college. I would have been too scared and wouldn't know how to start the process. Because it was local and so student-friendly, I felt I could do it." She uses her own example and stresses to faculty and staff that all need to be mentors.

She said, "One of the goals of the college is helping students and others build their self-esteem because that's what it did for me." She explained that about ninety-five percent of the students are Native American and over half of those getting their Bachelor's degree go on for their Master's. The primary value of tribal colleges in her view is the ability to mix Native American ideals and traditions in most of the courses. She said, "Students who come here are not only getting a good education in their field but they are learning of the Native American culture and language. So, they are really getting a double major. We try our best to practice our values, such as generosity, in our college. We, here at Sitting Bull College, can take the time."

At the Little Big Horn College on the Crow Reservation at Crow Agency, Montana, both Dr. David Yarlott and Dr. Lanny Real Bird

---

* A portrait of Sitting Bull can be seen in the administrative offices showing him wearing a Christian cross. He never converted but is said to have worn that as a statement that all religions come from the same source. This is in contrast to a monument near where he was killed that gives him faint praise and says he was a good, "but misguided leader."

started college there in its early days and returned to give back to the Reservation.

Yarlott, President of the college in 2009, said he left the Reservation to go to Western Montana College in Dillon. He said, "I lasted about a month."[38] In 1980 he heard about the opening of a college at the Crow Agency. He said, "It was an opportunity to pursue my college education without having to leave home. There was one office space and two classrooms." In 1989 he transferred to Montana State University in Bozeman, where he went on to a Master's and then a doctoral program.

As president of Little Big Horn College, he talked about the thrill of walking down the hallways these days and hearing faculty and students carrying on conversations in the Crow language.

In addition to a full range of academic study, student activities include going out as a group to kill and clean a buffalo, with the elders explaining the different parts of the buffalo, including their practical and spiritual significance. Following this, the students sit around the campfire and listen to the elders talk about the culture.

Lanny Real Bird was another early student. He has held various positions with the college over an eighteen-year period, starting out in finance. He had no experience and was unprepared, but it was a job that needed to be done, so he did it, and he said, "I learned on the job."[39]

His conviction about the importance of the college on the Reservation is strong and persistent. He has turned down many opportunities for more financially rewarding positions elsewhere. He stayed at the college because of his strong desire to give back to his tribe some of what he was given.

Through times of strife and harmony, conflict and resolution, crisis and victory, failures and successes, discouragement and acceptance, the fruit from the toil of Pat and others is compelling evidence of their value. It wasn't just Pat who contributed to the establishment of these colleges. There were others, who, if not like-minded, at least shared similar objectives. Their perseverance and persistence, drive and determination, and blood, sweat, and tears continue to pay off as more and more Indian students are able to attend and graduate from colleges located on their home Reservations.

VII

Freelance Years

The challenging and highly rewarding work at WICHE proved too narrow for Pat's interests. Even though she was at the pinnacle of her career, she resigned so she could work freely on a wider range of interests.

Earning a living was not a matter of concern for Pat. She had always been able to find work—from babysitting when she was a young girl, to part-time work even while in college, to supplementing family income. At this time she resumed teaching. Good paying positions were found as a lecturer in the History Department of the University of Denver and as an instructor in the Sociology Department of the University of Colorado.

While an excellent, highly acclaimed and popular teacher, she did not choose an academic career. She never let teaching, or any other means of earning a livelihood, interfere with her greater love—Native American self-determination. She dealt with a host of social justice concerns, legislation, and operating procedures that supported the ability of American Indians to have greater responsibility over their own affairs, and she was determined to reverse the entrenched paternalistic policies that limited Indian self-rule.

Even while living in Boulder and being involved with her many projects, her heart was on the Reservation. Not only did she return for the sun dance as often as she could, there were other concerns that pulled her to the Reservation. She and her sister owned some land that was being managed by others and she worried about how it was being used. She went to the real estate office of the Bureau of Indian Affairs in Ft. Yates, North Dakota to get some maps. Gerald (Jerry) Henrikson, who was in charge of the office, helped her identify her land. At that time he had no idea why she wanted the information or where that simple encounter would eventually lead. He soon learned the immediate problem. Someone in the Reservation Administration had taken it upon herself to lease their land to a white farmer without the knowledge or permission of the sisters who owned the land.

Pat quietly started the process of getting that situation reversed. She was still in Colorado, but her son, Kevin, was living on the Reservation. He did much of the onsite work to resolve the situation. Jerry, who thought he was just providing information, soon found himself in the middle of a dispute between two strong willed and determined Lakota women. Pat announced that henceforth she would take control of and responsibility for her own land. Jerry then had the task of informing the farmer that the deal that he thought he had for the land was null and void. It was rich fertile land, and the farmer wanted to raise wheat on it. Jerry, who was raised on a wheat farm, said it was some of the finest land on the Reservation for growing wheat. Pat would have none of that. She wanted it left for the wildlife. Ironically, she could have used the money as the subleasing would have greatly eased her financial situation. But she was determined that the land was to be left to nature. To this day, the land has never felt a plow. It is used for grazing cattle as well as a home for dear, rabbits, fox, and pheasants. It is land where the distinctive song of meadowlarks can be heard. Pat left much of the Reservation work and dealing with Jerry Henrikson to Kevin, as she was busy in Colorado and elsewhere. This resulted in building a strong bond between Kevin and the Henriksons.[40]

When Kevin was going to school at Black Hills State College (now Black Hills State University), his favorite teacher was Dr. Edwin Richardson. Pat met him later when Ed was teaching at the University of

Denver and Metropolitan State College. Ed is a Penobscot Indian from Maine with a distinguished military career. For a time he was teaching a course on counseling Indians suffering from alcoholism, while also conducting a private practice in psychology. Always on the lookout for suitable mentors for Kevin, Pat saw in Ed the qualities she wanted to influence her son, so she arranged for Kevin to come to Colorado to take another class from Ed, this time at the University of Denver. Close relationships were formed, and to this day Ed refers to Kevin as his son.[41]

Pat and Dr. Richardson attended conferences on Indian education, Indian counseling, and meetings of the National Congress for the American Indians. She called on him often over the years for help with Indians who were in trouble. He formed a club he called EIACT—Educating Indians to Appreciate their Culture and Traditions. Pat found him to be the perfect spokesperson to help Indians in trouble.

In talking about Pat, Ed would tick off her qualities in good academic style. He said, "One, she was very perceptive. Two, she was very sensitive, had a lot of feelings. Three, she was well organized. Some of our people aren't as organized as they might be, but she was. Four, she was extremely dedicated. Fifth, she was proud of her family, proud of her children. The sixth thing about her is she had good carry-through. If she said she was going to do something, she did it. A lot of people give you a commitment, but don't follow through. But she was really good at doing what she said she would do."

Of course, he didn't stop there. He went on to mention that she was extremely intelligent and that she was really good with people, especially those who are hard to get along with. He said she was classy while also being modest. She enjoyed singing Indian songs and was proud of her heritage.

The regard was mutual. Pat liked Ed's style. When an Indian was in trouble, he would go to the courthouse and ask the judge, "Can I see you in your chamber alone?" In the judge's chamber he would say, "I'm just a dumb psychologist, I don't know anything about law, but let me ask you some questions." Ed would ask the judge if he had a prejudice against longhaired Indians. Then he would watch for what psychologists call overreaction, which is a sure sign of prejudice.

Once he observed their reaction, he would know how to deal with the situation. He would say again that he didn't know anything about the law and that he was just a dumb psychologist and would ask questions that put him in charge of the conversation because it was not offensive. The result was that the Indian generally got more of a fair hearing than he would have had otherwise. Pat liked that style and would call on Ed often. This also illustrates the kind of networking that was a constant in Pat's life.

Another field of interest for Pat in the freelance years came from a cousin, Harriet Sky. They first met as adults, but formed a strong and enduring bond. In 1968 Harriet's father got a grant for an alcohol abuse workshop and Harriet was named coordinator. She said that first workshop was a complete disaster—even the keynote speaker got drunk. Harriet turned to Pat for solace, comfort, and advice. The two of them had serious talks about what went wrong and what could be learned from the experience. As a result of turning to Pat, the workshop became a learning experience and a launching pad for many highly successful alcohol abuse projects. Pat was not directly involved with these, but she was a constant source of wise counsel and inspiration throughout the time that Harriet was working in the field.

Harriet said that Pat's style was to write letters and use the telephone—she seemed to be constantly on the telephone. One time Harriet answered the phone and it was Pat calling from Tibet!

According to Harriet, Pat's greatest attribute was her capacity to care. When Harriet's fourteen-year-old son died, she had not notified Pat, but all of a sudden Pat silently appeared, standing at her side. During these darkest of hours Pat seemed to appear from nowhere, but there she was when comfort was needed most.[42]

The American Indian Religious Freedom Act
During the 1970s, while Pat was working with WICHE and AIHEC to establish tribal colleges, she was also working diligently on other projects. Most notable was the American Indian Religious Freedom

Act (Public Law 95-341).* She was marching up and down the halls of Congress for many causes related to American Indian rights. She used every tool at her command to try to change some of the prejudicial policies related to American Indians and Reservations, including her charismatic presence to enlist the aid of legislators.

Her efforts, along with the work of many other dedicated people, resulted in the enactment of the Act in 1978. The final language included many direct contributions from her drafts. Among other things the Act said ". . . it shall be the policy of the United States to protect and preserve for American Indians their inherent right to believe, express and exercise the traditional religions . . ." There was much rejoicing at the passage of the Act. It was documented recognition that American Indians are a worthy people with legitimate ways and traditions that are different from those of European descendants, whose beliefs dominate politics, life, and land, and marginalize the original inhabitants of this country.

One important provision in the Act stated that Indians should have access to sacred lands. Much of that land, especially in the Western states, was under the control of the government through the Forest Service, Bureau of Land Management, National Parks, or any of several other government agencies. Indians were not allowed access in many areas, never mind the centuries of traditional and sacred use. Among most Indian tribes, land is sacred and certain tracts especially so. This is in sharp contrast with the dominant culture that tends to regard land as a commodity to be exploited. Usage conflicts have been the inevitable result of these differing perspectives.

Especially disturbing was the denial of access to young Indian men to places considered important for their vision quests. Around the time of puberty, young men go off by themselves for a period of prayer and fasting. The purpose is to gain insight and guidance for

---

* Some cynics dismiss the whole act as an excuse for Indians to get high on peyote. That is somewhat like equating altar wine of the Christian Eucharist with drunkenness. Most Indians have little tolerance for those who misuse peyote, which is considered sacred and is often part of a vision quest.

their life. While missionaries had been unsuccessful in stopping the practice, the government made it much more difficult to carry out this rite of passage because its land policies denied access to places that were essential to the vision quest. The Act was a monumental step toward removing this and other obstacles to Indian self-identity.

It had been hard work, involving the tireless efforts of a lot of dedicated people. Pat had special praise for Senator Daniel Inouye, a Japanese-Hawaiian from Hawaii, who did so much for the Religious Freedom Act as well as other pieces of legislation of benefit to American Indians. Since the passage of the Act, Pat preferred the term "American Indian" to either Native American or Amerindian. In part this was a reflection of the legal language introduced by Senator Inouye, defining Indian rights and legal status.

Pat often formed a warm relationship with the members of Congress with whom she was working. With Senator Inouye there was mutual regard. He said of her: "Pat Locke was a true trailblazer who championed the rights of her people and fought tirelessly to ensure the rich cultural heritage and traditions of American Indians would be preserved and protected. Pat's unwavering commitment and countless contributions to the passage of the American Indian Religious Freedom Act of 1978 cemented American Indians' right to practice their spiritual faith. Her work and spirit live on through the traditions of her people and the tribal colleges she founded."[43]

She said of him that he was the embodiment of eloquence and brilliant declamation. He was always capable of dazzling listeners with his oratorical wizardry. Kevin said Pat liked to tell the story of a time when she and Senator Inouye were chatting just before he was to give a talk. Some people approached him and asked, "You speakie English?" He said he did and gave his talk. Afterward, he approached the ones who asked the questions and asked them, "I speakie OK?"

The Indians enjoyed ten years of protection under the Act until April 19, 1988 when the United States Supreme Court ruled that the U.S. Constitution does not protect American Indian religious practices, virtually canceling out the protection under the law and the years of hard work that Pat and others had put into gaining those rights.

The issue involved the Forest Service's intent to build a six-mile road through a site that had been held sacred for thousands of years by several Indian tribes in California. The purpose was to allow lumbering companies to harvest 733 million board feet of Douglas fir, even though a noninvasive route was available to the desired site.

The fight had gone on for years. A consortium of California Indian tribes filed suit against the Forest Service and prevailed in a lower court. The government appealed and the 9th Circuit Court of Appeals upheld the Indian's claim for protection on religious grounds. The government was not satisfied and appealed to the Supreme Court, which reversed the Court of Appeals decision by a split decision of five to three with one abstention. Pat was devastated.

Justice Sandra Day O'Connor wrote the majority opinion in the case known as the Chimney Rock-Lyng decision. At issue was the first amendment protection clause. O'Connor's opinion states that the government program did not prohibit the practice of religion even though it ". . . may make it more difficult to practice certain religions. . . ." The effective result was both a denial of the means of worshiping and a desecration of a sacred site. Since it did not coerce people to act contrary to their religious beliefs, she felt the government could build and pave the road anywhere it wanted. Mere prevention of practice did not seem sufficient in her opinion.

Justice Brennan wrote a sharply dissenting opinion, stating that the government action was a serious "restraint on religious practice" and was, indeed, a violation of first amendment protection. He noted that the Indians "have demonstrated that construction of the . . . road will completely frustrate the practice of their religion, for, as the lower courts found, the proposed logging and construction activities will virtually destroy respondents' (Indians') religion, and will therefore necessarily force them into abandoning those practices altogether."[44]

The decision reflected at least three subtle, but deep-seated prejudices. The first is that Indians were not considered Americans under the Constitution. They didn't gain citizenship in their own land until the Indian Citizenship Act of 1924. The second was that only

Abrahamic religions—Judaism, Christianity, and, to a lesser extent, Islam—were considered valid and legitimate. Indian ways and traditions were considered pagan by the missionaries and unlawful by legal definitions. The third was that because they did not use buildings such as a synagogue, church, or mosque in which to perform religious functions; their beliefs were not to be taken as seriously as organized religions and defended by law.

On May 4, 1988 Pat wrote an article for the *Mobridge Tribune* entitled, "Supreme decision denies Indian religion." In it she revealed the heartbreak she felt. She said: "I cannot describe the depths of sadness I feel about the Supreme Court's decision."

Pat concluded the article by saying, "It is ironic that Sandra O'Connor and the other four majority Justices are descendents of men and women who, suffering religious persecution in Europe, fled to this country, taking on our (Indian) protection so that they and their families could worship in their own way."[45]

Pat saw even deeper implications of this Supreme Court decision. If this decision prohibited Indians from certain practices of their religion, what is to protect other minority and little-understood religions? In Pat's thinking, it was a slap against religious freedom and put a lie to the promise of protection.

A short time after that Supreme Court decision, Pat was called to Washington as coordinator of a coalition of sixty-five organizations to rewrite the act. She was reluctant to attend for many reasons: she loved the Reservation and was getting tired of traveling; it was a favorite time of year and she was looking forward to the meadowlarks returning; and she felt it was time for others to take up the struggle.

The caller was not put off by any of these reasons and stressed that at issue was religious freedom requiring everyone's best efforts. The final, convincing argument was: "Pat, how can you think of sitting by the water when people are in agony."[46] So, once again, Pat drove the 100 miles to the airport and put her sense of duty for her people first.

It was sometimes hard for her to temper her bitterness over the Supreme Court's action. Eight years later, during a talk at Chautauqua in 1996, she said it was hard to live up to the meaning of her Lakota name, "Compassionate Woman," especially when she thought of Sandra Day O'Connor and that Supreme Court decision. She had to remind herself that O'Connor and the other four justices voting with the majority really could not be blamed. They were products of an American education system that glorified westward expansion. When Indians were mentioned at all, they were pictured as savages and obstacles to expansion. The vision of the justices was shaped by their education and culture.

As was so often the case, this setback generated new energy in Pat and she resolved to do two things. The first was to provide accurate information to white audiences. This she did tirelessly for the rest of her life. The other was to work even harder convincing tribes to control their own curricula so that Indian children could be taught their own heritage and not be insulted by the view prevalent in most history books that portrayed Indians as savage, subhuman villains. Indeed, she was convinced that Indian-controlled curricula were keys to Indian youth gaining a true appreciation of who they are and to realize the potential of their inherent gifts. The energy created by that Supreme Court decision knew no bounds.

Language Preservation[47]

Among the causes she was championing at this time was language preservation. The eventual creation of the Lakota Language Consortium was a realization of one of Pat's dreams as a hope for Lakota revitalization. Harlene Green, a Cherokee Indian from Oklahoma, had been writing grants and directing programs to save the Cherokee language. Her organization, Native American Language Issues Institute, supported all languages.

It was while seeking grants for language preservation that she met Pat and soon learned that Pat was a solid ally. As she said, "If you were on her side, you were her friend."

Both women felt a little deprived because they had not learned their respective languages from childhood and therefore felt they had been denied a part of their heritage. Both were determined to provide the legacy of language for future generations.

Another passionate American Indian language preservation advocate was LaDonna Harris of Albuquerque. The three of them worked together and became a force to be reckoned with. As Harlene said, "What Pat couldn't do, LaDonna could."

Harlene said they lobbied for languages, Pat in Washington and Harlene from home. They kept in touch and Pat would tell Harlene to call the Senators and Congressmen she had worked with, especially if there was a Congressman who was giving her a problem. Pat would have Congressmen who were sympathetic to language preservation talk to the ones who were obstacles.

They would talk to people around the country to bring pressure on certain representatives. She would find out who was doing what and use that information. Pat had a knack for making friends with the right people. Coretta Scott King was among her good friends and used her network and contacts in Washington to assist Pat in her work.

Pat didn't quarrel, demonstrate, or get involved with protests. Before getting into a situation, Pat always did her homework and even people who did not agree with her recognized and respected that. She did her work in Washington armed with hard facts, insight, and compelling logic. But she never gave the idea that she was smarter or knew more than anyone else. Pat was such a good lobbyist because she was normally nonconfrontational and lighthanded. However, she could be bold and intimidating, if that was needed. She would speak directly to a Congressman and say, "This is what we want you to do." Often the response was a put-off, such as he had to think about it or just that he would not do it. Pat would say, "No, I want a promise and this is why." Then she would outline issues from his home district and why it would be politically to his advantage to do as she said. She had her facts in order and was highly effective. Almost singlehandedly she got a bill passed that children should not be forced to speak a language other than their own.

In describing Pat's style Harlene said that, "She could be meaner than hell and sweet as pie. I've seen her walk into a Congressional office with four or five women with their arms folded across their chests and Pat would say, 'Now listen, damn it. These ladies and I have decided that we need your help and this is what we expect you to do. If you don't believe it, ask them,' and we would just stand there with our arms crossed." She did the talking, but there was no question in the Congressman's mind that he was up against a solid front.

She talked about the law and the Constitution and how her request related to those things he was concerned about. She told Harlene, "They work for me." If she didn't like what they were doing she would say, "They aren't working for me any longer." She knew every committee and she didn't deal with the weaker Congressmen—she went to the strong ones.

If that didn't work out, the three women would take the next step. They would go back to the Congressman's home district and find someone close to him to get his cooperation. If that didn't work, they were not above working to defeat uncooperative legislators in the next election.

In Harlene's estimate, the most memorable things about Pat were her tenacity, stubbornness, and love for her family. She observed, "I have never seen Pat work for anything personally. She loved Indian people from whatever tribe and she would work hours a day to try to do things, but nothing for herself. If there was a mother who couldn't get something her baby needed because of a bureaucratic problem, Pat would be like a tiger, but never for herself.

"She made me strong. She made me know that I could be strong. She made me feel the rights of others and what was important. She made me know that Indian people are still being treated badly in some areas of this country. She opened my eyes to some of the inequalities that are going on right here in Oklahoma. I hadn't paid any attention before, but Pat made me stop and think about inequalities. If she saw something wrong in your tribe she would tell you, if it made you mad that was all right, but she didn't make people feel bad in the process. She would say this is what you can do about it if you want to and it was never militant. She was one who could talk and negotiate and she would make sense to the people working in the Office of Civil Rights."

In addition to their work together for language preservation, Harlene spoke about Pat's personality and the effect she had on others. Harlene said she never saw anyone who didn't like Pat and have a great deal of respect for her.

Harlene said, "The way she looked at you—Oh, my! I have seen her sit down at a table with a number of people and soon everyone would be looking at her. The way she dressed and the way she talked, she could just burn a hole in you."

Many people have mentioned her clothing and the way she carried herself. She would wear simple, inexpensive garments and when she wore them, they looked regal. A simple scarf or wrap would put an elegant and sophisticated touch on her presence. When meeting people, looking like a queen, having vast knowledge and competence, made her a formidable advocate of whatever she was trying to accomplish.

Harlene concluded talking about Pat by saying how much she missed her, "Sometimes I want to talk to her. Sometimes I talk out loud to her. Doing that, I think I know how she would answer me and that gives me the strength to go ahead and do something. I sure do miss her. I called Kevin the other night because I needed to ask Pat a question. He's a lot like her and he helped me out a lot. I lost my husband in November and I miss Pat almost as much as I do him. She would have made a good president."

Pat never put on airs. She was always herself. At high-level meetings she would often sneak out the back door, as she said, "To smoke a cigarette with the cab drivers." During one high level meeting on language preservation she was being her usual self with cab drivers who came from different parts of the world. They were talking and laughing about how all their friends were trying to get them to quit smoking, as if they didn't already know the dangers of it. One gentleman asked her nationality. He asked if she knew Kevin Locke and she admitted that she did. He then insisted that she come with Kevin to the Marshal Islands where Kevin was to perform. She dismissed it as an offhand comment by a cab driver only to discover later that he was the Prime Minister of the Marshal Islands and the featured speaker of the program, and that this was a serious invitation in the curling smoke among the cab drivers. So she went with Kevin to the Marshal Islands.

This was but one of many trips throughout the Pacific on behalf of language preservation. Her hard work for the preservation of indigenous languages everywhere was well noted. In 1999 she was elected President of Pacific and American Indigenous Language Survival, Inc.

During one of her many trips among the Maoris she was introduced to some people and she shook hands in the formal, traditional Lakota way: a light touch with one short and brief pump. She noticed some suppressed snickers that she didn't understand. Later, much to her embarrassment, she learned that among the Maoris, shaking hands in that manner was a sign from a woman of ill-repute saying she was available.

Preservation of Sacred Sites [48]

Gary Kimble is a Gros Ventres Indian from Fort Belknap, Montana. He earned his law degree from the University of Montana and in 1972 was elected to the Montana State Legislature. At that time there were few Indians in elected positions. He first met Pat while doing some consulting work in Washington, D.C. As a practicing lawyer and State Legislator interested in higher education for Indians he would run into Pat often and got to know and respect her.

Gary worked on a project for the protection of sacred sites in New York. When a vacancy in the staff occurred, he asked Pat to take it. Much of the important work she did while there is documented in a library on the Association on American Indian Affairs at Princeton.

Gary was the first Indian director for the project. Others who had been working on the project were archaeologists or historians whose primary purposes were academic. Gary asked Pat to join him in his work and together they changed the focus. Their emphasis was the preservation of ceremonial sites so traditional people could perform their sacred rites.

Gaining access to the sites was one thing. There was an even larger issue. That was protection against multiple use of the land. The objective was to stop logging or grazing on the sacred sites so they would be undisturbed. That met with a lot of resistance from the logging companies, counties, and states involved with the land in question. In the conflict between economic development and religious rites, economic development usually wins. Sometimes, depending on the attitude, getting permission from the government agencies could be an even bigger problem than working with industry leaders. When the differences involved bureaucratic power struggles and territorial disputes, the challenges loomed large.

Gary and Pat worked with many organizations and agencies, including the Medicine Wheel Coalition that was attempting to protect the medicine wheel, a big circle of rocks in the Bighorn Mountains in Wyoming. The intention was to make sure grazing of cattle didn't hurt the site, and that Indians could continue to use it undisturbed. It was necessary to get agreement from the Forest Service, the Bureau of Land Management, and sometimes the people who had the grazing leases as well as county, state, and federal agencies.

It was complicated by the difficulty of getting consensus among the twenty to thirty tribes that used the land. There were often wide differences as to how the land should be treated in a traditional sense. So the first problem was to reach a consensus among the tribes. Then they would start negotiating with the agencies and wait for years and years until it all came together. There were no quick successes.

Phone calls between Gary and Pat were common. Gary reported that he would call her and say, "Pat, what are you doing?" She would say, "Well, I'm sitting here thinking." He thought that was such a profound statement. He said, "She was a really, really creative thinker. She always tried to seek solutions to things. So I knew that she was working hard when she'd say, 'I'm just sitting here thinking.' And I knew something big was going to happen."

As with many of her projects, being involved with one thing would lead to another challenge. Mount Graham, Arizona is a sacred site and Pat worked with Catherine Davis for its preservation. It was also an ideal location for a telescope and work was going forward for the Telescope Columbus project. An organization was formed called the Apache Survival Coalition for Mount Graham to stop developing that sacred site for the telescope. They were not successful. The telescope was built, although it involved a clear and severe violation of sacred land. The group became philosophical. They had confidence that in the long run the mountain would protect itself.

Gradually their concern over sacred sites developed into a worldwide vision. Gary and Pat discovered common problems in South America. They met a man from Bolivia who was concerned because the sacred sites in the Andes were being protected for archaeological purposes and not for ceremonial purposes. Once again Pat's interest and sound advice went beyond political boundaries.

An aspect of their sacred sites projects was getting federal legislation to repatriate funerary objects that were in museums and private collections so they could go back to traditional people. So there was always scrutiny of museums' collections, so that sacred and traditional items could be repatriated to the tribes that wanted them. As an example, the Museum of the American Indians, located in Washington, D.C., had items that were ceremonial in character that some tribes wanted back and they couldn't always get them.

Another matter that Pat and Gary worked on had to do with Indians who were in prison. They felt that imprisoned Indians should have the right to religious freedoms even while incarcerated. There was little problem of allowing medicine men to come into the prisons and talk to inmates. That seemed harmless.

Problems arose when the Indians wanted to have sweat lodges. That was hard for prison authorities to accept. There was an ingrained reluctance to allow Indians to go into an enclosure alone or with a medicine man for an hour or two to pray in the sweat lodge without prison personnel being present, or to have one prison guard alone in an enclosure with several Indians. Even being armed, they could be overpowered. Prison authorities just did not like it. But it was a battle that Pat and Gary took on with some failures and a few successes.

Gary commented on Pat's charm and her unusual ways of keeping others just a little off balance. He said, "Sometimes when she came to New York in the winter we'd be all bundled up with a top coat and gloves and a hat and Pat would come strolling into the restaurant in her elegant way without a coat. I remember it was colder than hell in Greenwich Village. We had gone to my favorite Italian restaurant and the rest of us had huge coats on and muffs and hats and gloves and top coats. Pat came striding in without a coat. I said, 'Are you sure you're not cold?' She said, 'No, Gary. I never am cold. I have a high set point for body heat.'" Kevin agreed. He said she would always sleep with her window open even when it was thirty degrees below zero outside.

Such were some of the trials and tribulations during her free-lance years for causes about which she cared so deeply. While she accomplished much, her wide-ranging activities and busy life on matters of concern to Indians served but to fuel her desire to live on the Reservation.

VIII

Reservation Life

Busy as she was with her many projects, Pat was not satisfied. She wanted life on a Reservation. She was enjoying success, had a nice house in Boulder, Colorado with handy access to airports for her frequent travels, but it was not a Reservation. By right of ancestry she could move either to the White Earth Reservation in Minnesota—home of her Chippewa father, or to the Standing Rock Reservation, spanning North and South Dakota—home of her Lakota mother. Her son, Kevin, was already living on Standing Rock and she wanted to be near her grandchildren.

Mobridge, South Dakota, the principal community near the Reservation, is nestled along the eastern bank of Lake Oahe. It is a commercial center for the surrounding area of ranches, rolling hills, and the Reservation. The Standing Rock Reservation—home of Lakota Indians—is on the west bank of the lake with a bridge for U.S. Highway 12 spanning the lake and connecting Mobridge to the Reservation. While *Oahe* means *foundation,* the lake is not a foundation for understanding, nor is the bridge a bridge of acceptance. The lake is a chasm and the bridge a wall.

The lake was named after the Oahe Mission, which had been built on the foundation of an old trading post. The dam forming the lake was built in 1948 for power generation in central South Dakota. The resulting lake took away over 200,000 acres of prime agriculture land from the Cheyenne River and Standing Rock Indian Reservations. The loss of this land had a dramatic effect on the Indians living there. One visitor to the Reservations asked why there were so few older Indians and was told that "the old people had died of heartache" because of the construction of the dam and the loss of the Reservations' land.*

Mobridge and the Reservation may be a short distance apart geographically, but they are leagues apart by culture and customs. Halfway across the lake there is a sign noting the change of time between Central and Mountain Time Zones. Symbolic of the chasm is the fact that the Lakota ignore the time change. The Reservation is geographically in the Mountain Time Zone, but Lakota clocks are on Central Time. So, Indians and non-Indians, west of Lake Oahe, living side by side—and sometimes under the same roof—remain an hour apart by the clock. And many are even further apart in their views of life.

The bridge allows travelers to speed across the water on U.S. Highway 12, oblivious of the contrasting lives surrounding it. On a hill overlooking the bridge stands the Grand River Casino, which is owned by the Reservation and effectively extracts money, mainly from white clients whose forefathers took these lands a century and a half ago. Most casino customers remain indifferent to the Reservation and its people. Turning to the north, just past the bridge, is the road leading into the Standing Rock Reservation. There is another bridge, called the "singing bridge," over an arm of Lake Oahe. Road noise from the bridge sounds like a welcoming serenade of Lakota singing.

There are goodhearted people who love their children and want the best for them living on both sides of this great divide. While there are people who respect and have high regard for people living on the

---

* See Michael L. Lawson's *Dammed Indians: the Pick-Sloan Plan and the Missouri River Sioux, 1944–1980,* University of Oklahoma Press, 1982.

other side, there are also those who don't understand and are suspicious or even contemptuous of the others.

An example of conflicting views from opposite sides is the way the local weekly paper, the *Mobridge Tribune,* is perceived. People in Mobridge had complained that it was becoming an Indian paper. On the other side of the river, people complained that the *Tribune* ignores Indians and the Reservation.

In 1983, when Pat was about 55, she sold her house in Boulder, and with the proceeds moved to the Mobridge area with her daughter, Winona, and Winona's three children. First they lived in a tent a few miles from Mobridge, not far from the house she got later. They then left their tent for a rental in Mobridge. Kevin and his family moved to within two blocks of them.

Pat's move was not easy. Her freelance consulting work involved frequent travel, and she had to drive at least 100 miles either to Bismark, North Dakota or to Aberdeen, South Dakota to fly to wherever she was going.

Money was scarce. The sale of her house in Boulder paid for her move with a little money left over. That money, together with her freelance work, which was uncertain, is what they lived on. While her travels were sometimes paid by organizations that wanted her presence, and she occasionally got paid for consulting work, frequently she used her own meager resources to attend something about which she felt strongly. Sometimes it was a choice between travel and personal necessities. An example of her frugal ways is reflected in her discovery and use of a copy machine in Mobridge that was malfunctioning to the point of giving two copies for the price of one.

Kevin had gotten a house on the Reservation in January of 1987 and Pat wanted to be near her grandchildren. In a touching letter to the Lakota Tribal Council, she explained why she wanted to take advantage of her Hunkpapa Lakota heritage and live on the Standing Rock Reservation.

The Tribal Council made land available on a beautiful spot, just past the singing bridge, on a high point overlooking two arms of

Lake Oahe and just across the main Reservation road from Kevin. Two or three years after Kevin got his house, Pat, Winona, and her children got their house. It was a modest but adequate house with a breathtaking view.

The Reservation was where she wanted to be. When asked why she wanted to live on the Reservation in South Dakota rather than some place more convenient for her many travels, she would answer simply, "It's home." As was typical, that simple answer implied much more. It contained her commitment to cultural and language preservation, her compassion for improving the lot of her people at the grassroots level while also working aggressively for improvement through available agencies, as well as serving as a natural balm for her soul.

The absorbing life of the Reservation increased her passion for language and cultural preservation, Indian rights, and education— all of which were aimed toward enabling Indian youth to become engaged with the wider world without sacrificing their heritage.

She also vigorously continued to pursue her other causes: women's rights, the environment, and anything else she viewed as abuses of basic human rights. In so doing, she was actively involved with a number of groups in support of her aims, usually in a leadership role. These included being Director of the Education Components of the National Tribal Chairmen's Association. They advised and gave technical support to tribal education programs. She was also the Education Project Director of the National Congress of American Indians. In this capacity she was involved in research in American Indian post-secondary education.

She delighted in inviting people from various agencies to her home. Many people dealing with Indian affairs had only a superficial taste of Reservation life. In addition to her natural and gracious hospitality, she wanted people dealing with Indian matters to have the experience of being on a Reservation and meeting people who actually lived there. She often called for high-level meetings to be held at her home so they could experience the beauty, the remoteness, the simplicity, and the tranquility of Reservation life for themselves.

In addition to all that, she loved to be there: to be with her grand-children and take part in their activities; to be with her many dogs; to interact with her people; to take part in powwows, celebrations, and festivals; to see, hear, smell, taste, and feel the changes of seasons; to hear the singing of the many birds, especially the distinctive song of the meadowlark; to watch the deer and an occasional fox or coyote romping through the brush on the water's bank; to revive her spirit; and just to think.

Yes, it was home, with all the varied and subtle implications of that simple word.

IX

Her Family[49]

Nothing held a higher place in Pat's heart than her family. Deep and ardent as her passions were for Indian education, language preservation, rights for Indians and women, the environment, worldwide indigenous rights, and so on, they paled in comparison to the adoration she felt for her children and grandchildren. She felt keenly that families were like glue holding societies, cultures, and, in fact, the whole world together.

Even though her marriage to Ned Locke ended in divorce, she never spoke ill of him and encouraged the children to maintain good relationships with their father. Kevin spent his junior year in high school with him in Virginia, while Winona stayed at home with her mom.

Pat's love was sensitive to differences, open and generous, and accepting of people as they were, not as she thought they should be. As mentioned earlier, when Kevin and Winona were young, she always arranged work so the children could be with her. She was constantly looking for ways to enrich their experiences.

After high school, Pat arranged for both children to go to the Haskell Art Institute as well as the Santa Fe Art Institute. Both children met future spouses while at school. As a special delight for Pat, each family produced three grandchildren whom she adored and on whom she doted lavishly.

From about 1969 through 1983, Pat lived in Boulder, Colorado. As for her family, Winona's marriage dissolved, and she and her three children moved in with Pat. The four of them became a single family. Mother and daughter worked closely together as Winona would often type for her mother, help prepare material, and would even draft speeches for Pat or others. The two of them would talk a great deal about Pat's projects. It was after a trip to Alaska that conversations with Winona gave birth to her passion for tribal colleges with tribal control of the curricula.

The two of them would talk about ways to get better education for the Reservations and how to help organizations, such as the National Tribal Leaders Association or the National Congress of American Indians, improve in order to accomplish the work so dear to Pat's heart. Most of the leadership in these organizations was male. These two women would figure out the best way to operate with the situation as it was. Their strategies paid off. Pat was often elected to leadership positions in these traditionally male-dominated organizations. Innovative, driven, and creative as she was, she never did anything against the culture.

While Kevin appreciated and supported the work his mother was doing, he took an independent path. He turned to Abraham End of Horn as a mentor and father figure. Abraham said, "I remember him writing me when he was in high school saying, 'I'm thinking of going to college but I'm just not sure that's the right thing for me to do. I just maybe want to spend some time among Indian people.'"[50]

When Kevin graduated from high school, he knew only a few Lakota words. He went to the Reservation to spend time with Abraham and other older people. He set a goal of learning seventeen Lakota words per day. Today he is noted as one of the most fluent second-language Lakota speakers.* Abraham went on to explain

---

* Kevin's proficiency in the Lakota language is such that Floyd Westerman, who played the part of Ten Bears in the movie "Dances with Wolves," would call on Kevin for advice on the pronunciation and usage of Lakota words.

Pat, Kevin, and Winona in their formal Indian clothing

how Pat wanted to make sure that Kevin had a good education, both among people who could be mentors, helping him to learn the Native ways, and as someone who could be successful in the white man's world.

Pat had suggested that Kevin go to law school and he tried it. Within a few weeks he realized that his interests were elsewhere and he switched to studying Native music and education. Typical of her trust in her children, she wholeheartedly supported his choice.*

Kevin attended several schools, including the Black Hill State College, but graduated from the University of North Dakota with a teaching degree. After receiving his teaching degree, he returned to the Standing Rock Reservation as a teacher. While he could have had more lucrative positions elsewhere, he was concerned there were too few Indians teaching Indians and he felt that it was important for him to teach on the Reservation.

At that time most of the teachers were white and did not live on the Reservation. Many of these teachers were condescending, patronizing, or contemptuous. As soon as school was out at the end of the day, many would race home because they were afraid to be on the Reservation after dark. Kevin stayed on the Reservation and started his family there.

He would frequently go to Boulder to see his mom and he kept encouraging her to return to the Reservation, which she did often, especially during sun dances. Kevin's oldest daughter, Kimimila, called her grandmother "Airport Unchi" because she thought that's where Pat lived. She would go with her dad when he would drive to the airport in Bismark or Aberdeen to pick up her grandmother. So, naturally, that is where she thought she lived. Kevin helped Pat in many ways in matters dealing with Reservation issues.

Teaching never interfered with Kevin's love for powwows. While Kevin was attending the Black Hills State College in 1972, Harley and Debbie Goodbear, who came from a well-known Indian dancing family, came to an event where Kevin met them. Later, Harley invited Kevin to go on a tour with them, which he did.

Harley's brother, Arlo Goodbear, thought Kevin could be a hoop dancer and offered to give him four lessons. He told him, "If you do

---

* It was left to a granddaughter, Maymangwa Flying Earth-Miranda, to become the first lawyer in the family.

your part on this dance you will meet many people and see many people and have many experiences. But you have to do your part."[51]

Kevin was given about fifteen minutes of basic instruction on designs. About a week later, when he was back on the Reservation, he got a call from the Goodbear family. Arlo had been in an accident and was killed. Kevin was asked to be one of the pallbearers. After the funeral, he had a series of vivid dreams in which he saw Arlo dancing.

The dreams gave Kevin a sense of the spiritual significance of the dance—he'd hear the song, then see a light and see Arlo dancing. It seemed as if Arlo was restoring his place in the hoop of life. Kevin saw people who were downcast. Arlo would dance and the light would build and create designs, like a flower. In Kevin's thinking, the dream fulfilled the lessons Arlo had promised. It seemed to be the completion of a covenant. The dreams were a symbolic manifestation of a spiritual reality: the potential all of us have is dormant; through dancing the spirit can come out. The hoop symbolized the interrelationship and interdependence of all of life. Kevin felt a sense of mission to convey this spiritual conviction. He does not see himself as a dancer teaching spiritual values, but as an educator using dance as his medium of instruction.

The U.S. State Department had scheduled Arlo to go on a two-month tour to Senegal, Ghana, and Congo in West Africa. Since Arlo had been killed before final preparations were made, they asked his mother who could go in his place. She recommended Kevin. He was hesitant. He didn't want to say no and he didn't want to say yes. He finally said he would try. On that tour he developed, refined, and perfected his dance routine. It was the launching of his career as an internationally acclaimed performer, furthering, through the arts, his means of teaching the objectives his mother was pursuing through her activism. He still loves to teach from the dancing platform.

Dorothy Locke, Kevin's former wife, said she was with Pat when people would find out they were from South Dakota. They would ask them if they knew Kevin Locke. Dorothy said that Pat would look at her and say, "We know him." Then she would look at them and say, "And we know his mother and his sister and his wife."[52] She would let it go at that.

Over the years Pat and Kevin often traveled together, each with an intense but different agenda: Pat would meet with indigenous and government leaders, and Kevin would put on his performance. A constant with their travels was having one or more of Pat's grandchildren with them. While the purposes of the trips were serious, as far as the grandchildren were concerned they were fun trips with Unchi and / or Dad. Kimimila reported that by the time she was twenty-four she had been to twenty-four countries. And all that time she never had a clue as to what her grandmother was doing because "Unchi" never focused on herself, just on the grandchildren.

Kevin, however, incorporated Kimimila into his dance routines. So, father and daughter danced their way through many parts of the world. In 1993 he invited her to go on a tour with him that conflicted with her high school graduation. Without any pressure he let her decide. She went on the dancing tour throughout Asia and missed her own graduation.

Pat insisted that when the grandchildren traveled with her it was not just for the purpose of sightseeing. She wanted them to meet the local people and understand their cultures. It's no wonder that when asked about her grandmother, Waniya answered, "She was not like a typical grandmother. Wherever we were in the world, we got to see different cultures and families."[53] She mentioned being among the Maoris in New Zealand, walking the beaches and eating popcorn in Brazil, and many other international excursions that were just part of life.

While living across the highway from Kevin, every morning at nine o'clock Pat would call Kevin's house to see how his children were doing. The ten members of the extended family spent much time together. The three children from each family would meet at the highway and go to school together—all this to Pat's utter delight. And the grandchildren remain close as they have grown up. Even today they sometimes refer to their cousins as brothers or sisters.

For Pat, her bedroom was her office and her bed was her desk. There were piles and piles of papers on her bed, and a small area where she would sleep. There was a narrow pathway winding through her research material to the bed. When one of the grandchildren would walk in, work would stop and the grandchildren would become the focus of her attention.

There was a small television in the corner of the room. Sometimes it was on while she worked, either playing news or sports. That's all she watched. She watched sports, especially basketball, so she could better talk with her grandsons, Duta, Hepana, and Ohiyes'a, and the many other boys hanging around the house. She had no interest in soap operas, sitcoms, game shows, or anything else on TV.

Pat loved to cook for the two families. Any accomplishment was reason for a feast—high grades, a good report from school, athletic achievements, or whatever other special hallmark was reached. And her meals were like holiday banquets. Once a month or more she would fix lavish meals for her family.

One morning, the six grandchildren were fighting about something. Pat never liked to see the children squabbling, so she put a stop to it. She fixed breakfast and made them all sit there and eat it in silence as a reminder that they were not to fight. The lesson is well recalled these many years later.

That was similar with the way she dealt with her own frustrations—in silence and contemplation. Working for change is a powerful magnet for criticism, conflict, and contention. Disappointment, setbacks, and frustrations are part of the process, but she was not one to lash out in anger. When things were not going well she would be quiet, and she would cook and fuss over her many and omnipresent dogs. She wanted her grandchildren to be able to control their frustrations as well.

When Kimimila was asked what stood out to her about her grandmother, she replied: "The fact that she cared for us so much. When she was alive, I didn't even realize all of the things that she was doing. When she was with us, her whole focus was on us. She would cook for us. She was an amazing cook. After she served us, she would sit down and just watch us eat. She would say, 'I just like to watch you guys eat and watch you guys enjoy the food.' She would eat after we were done.

"When my dad and I would go on tours, she would pack little packages of raisins and things to make sure that we had something to eat. Her whole focus was on us and doting on us and caring for us. I remember that she would sing lullabies to us. While she sang she would make circles around our eyes with her fingers; like rubbing our foreheads and our cheeks and stuff and making circles like a figure eight. It was real soothing."[54]

Her love was complete and unconditional. When Kimimila got pregnant without being married, she was embarrassed and did not want to face her grandmother. Pat's reaction came as a surprise. She said, "Oh, good. I am so happy." There was never a word about marital status. And she followed every step of the pregnancy with joy and excitement. She would call almost daily asking how she was, how the baby, still in the womb, was doing. When it came time for delivery there were twelve relatives in the delivery room with Kimimila: Pat, Kimimila's dad, mother, aunt, brother, sister, and cousins. The doctor kept saying that only two people were allowed, but they paid no attention. Kimimila claims her daughter, Anpao, "was born into a spiritual and prayerful environment. My mom held her, my dad held her, and then my grandmother held her."

When Anpao was in diapers, Pat would give her a hose and ask her to water the garden. Naturally, she made a lot of mud to play in and Pat would roll up her pants and play in the mud with her great-granddaughter.

Kimimila got an apartment in Mobridge and her grandmother came to see the baby as often as she could. That was in 1998 and Pat decided Kimimila needed a car. One day, without any previous discussion, she announced they were going to look for a car. Pat paid $500 for an '85 Chrysler New Yorker. Practical as she was, before closing the deal, she had a mechanic look at it, to make sure granddaughter and great-granddaughter would be safe. When Kimimila went back to college in Albuquerque, she would drive the 1,100 miles back home whenever she could. The car served her well and without trouble for two years.

Kimimila went on about her grandmother, "I never realized that she was unusual. When she passed in 2001 and I started reading the articles written about her, I felt like a complete idiot because I never realized all of the things that she had done. She never spoke about it. None of those things ever came out in a discussion or anything that we were talking about. When we would come home from college she would always ask, 'What are you doing?' or, 'How are you doing? What are you studying? What did you learn?' It wasn't, 'I did this and this.'"

On the other hand, Pat spoke often, freely, and lovingly about her grandchildren with her colleagues. Even when they were in the midst of intense battles with Congressmen in Washington, D.C., colleagues who had never met her grandchildren felt they knew them because Pat spoke of them so often.

While firm with the grandchildren, she was also protective. Waniya said as the youngest she was spoiled and would talk back. Her parents would try to stop her, but her grandmother would intervene and say, "No, she needs to have that voice." Waniya was still in high school when she got pregnant and wanted to drop out and get her GED. Pat would not hear of it. Working with the school, she made arrangements for mother and son, Ohitika, to continue in school with a babysitter who would get Waniya out of class when the baby needed feeding.

It was when Waniya was working and going to school at Sitting Bull College in Ft. Yates, North Dakota, that she realized how much her grandmother had done in so many ways. The school may not have been there if it wasn't for her grandmother. She said, "Every time I walk into the college I appreciate what she did—having a state of the art college on the Reservation. If there wasn't a school on Standing Rock, I could never go to college."

When the grandchildren were away in college, Pat would plan her frequent trips in such a way that she could see them en route to wherever she was going. Maymangwa reported special meetings she had with her grandmother between flights at an airport. Her grandmother was filled with both tender loving concern and practical advice. One time when Maymangwa had been part of a political rally and protest, Pat told her that was a waste of time. If she wanted to get things done she had to go to Washington and talk directly to the decision-makers.[55]

Pat's grandson, Hepana, was living in Manderson on the Pine Ridge Indian Reservation and would drive to Wakpala often to see his family. Late one night, while driving back to Wakpala, there was an accident and he was killed. It was 1999 and Pat was devastated. He had been with her since he was a small child, when his mother, Winona, and his sister and brother moved in with her. Pat dealt with his death with an outward stoicism that belied the intense grief that she felt. She turned her attention to the work yet to be done. She plunged back into her work, but her heart was heavy. According to Kevin she never quite recovered, but she carried on as best she could.

X

Friends and Neighbors

Pat cherished life on the Reservation. Every year, even prior to moving there, whenever possible she would attend the Sitting Bull sun dance held early in July. As mentioned in Chapter II, her parents would take her to Indian rituals as a small child even though they were illegal at that time and their jobs could have been in jeopardy. Now, after the passage of the Indian Religious Freedom Act, on which Pat had worked so hard, Indian rituals could be performed legally. She always held her head high, but it must have been an especially thrilling experience for her to attend the sun dance after the passage of the act.

She found a special bounty on the Reservation. She was close to her two children and six grandchildren; had a safe environment for her many dogs; had access to a good library, which she used liberally; and could spend more time with the friends and relatives she had come to know over the years.

In addition to her travels and continued work for Indian rights, she became an integral part of two different worlds right at home—both the activities of the Reservation, and that of the mostly white community of Mobridge, which was across the river from the Reservation. With her special ways and regal presence Pat was highly regarded by many people on both sides of the river. Yet she was unassuming and humble. She neither placed herself above others nor was she intimidated by anyone, regardless of their rank in life. She preferred to be known simply as Unchi. She was often called that and it was a role she loved to fill.

Many people from the Standing Rock Reservation came to know and admire her before she moved there, because she had been a fixture at the sun dances. The purpose of the sun dance is to strengthen both individuals and the culture. People have said that talking to Pat during the ceremonies added a dignity, strength, and wisdom to the sacred occasion.

People from the Reservation speak of Pat with a respect that borders on awe. They mention her intelligence, wisdom, and vast experience. But more often they say how much she cared, and speak of the impact she made on people's lives.

With characteristic vigor she entered into Reservation life. Jesse Taken Alive was the tribal chairman at the time and there had been an interest in setting up a radio station. Pat not only became a force behind the project, but she was on the first board of directors and continued to serve on the radio's board for the rest of her life. Taken Alive was also a member of the board and he would rave about how much she contributed with her broad outlook and vast experience.[56]

A distant relative, Robert End of Horn, Sr., had been close to her since they were teenagers, but they didn't learn that they were related until later. They called each other cousins although they were probably second or third cousins. He said that over the years he had never known Pat to get mad or upset. He said, "She always had a chuckle in her voice." Frequently, with his boys, he would go to her house and the boys would do yardwork for her. He would laugh about her love for dogs and quote Kevin as saying his mother's house was "dog heaven." People from Mobridge would let their dogs loose and they would often find their way to her house.[57]

Robert's boys have no end of praise for Unchi.[58] They would go to her house to help with the yardwork or just hang out. When she would go on her frequent trips, they would stop by the house to make sure everything was all right. She loved to feed them. Robert, Jr. said she taught them how to cook, especially soup. Now, whenever he makes soup, he thinks of Unchi and hopes it will be good enough.

While not a basketball fan, Pat would watch basketball with the boys on TV and learned a lot about the sport, just so she could talk to them about something they liked. She would attend their games when they were playing for Wakpala high school and cheer them on.

Her guidance and encouragement was always gentle with a touch of humor. Several of the boys loved to tell of the time they were watching something blatantly sexy on MTV. She just said, "Turn that off. It's like watching a bunch of dogs mating out there." They laughed, turned it off, and delighted in recalling it years later.

They all credit Pat for encouraging them in whatever they are doing, especially education. When Stoney End of Horn wanted to go into the Marine Corps, she clearly voiced her preference for him to get an education instead. In part because she felt that being in the service created an appetite for war and violence. In contrast to that she told him that knowledge is power. He thought she meant political power and he wasn't interested. He decided to join the Marines. Pat disagreed, but supported him in his decision. It wasn't until he was in bootcamp that he understood what she meant by glorifying war. Later he learned what she really meant about knowledge being power. He was stationed in Japan when he learned that his beloved Unchi died. He took two weeks of leave so he could have time by himself to grieve. Now, out of service, he is following her advice and seeking a degree in architecture.

Earl Medicine had a different story to tell. As a single parent, a father of four daughters, he was at a loss about how to be a good father. His father told him that he had to learn how to raise his daughters from experienced and honorable women. While not physically related to Pat, and even though there were older women who were his relatives, he turned to Unchi for guidance. "One of my fondest memories was sitting in her home with all her dogs and her telling me stories and what our role was as warriors*—just talking as grandson and grandma, and she would talk to me about doing more for

---

* See Chapter III for the Lakota meaning of warrior.

our people. A lot of time I wanted to move into the city because I'm an artist and there is a better market in the city, but she would tell me of the importance of relating stories to the younger people. I wanted my daughters to be like her. Because of Unchi's influence, one of them is now working on her Master's degree."[59]

Earl is a successful artist. With inspiration from Pat he formed a corporation on the Reservation with his sister, and they won a million dollar contract for producing items for the Lewis and Clark Centennial. While working on the project, they were able to provide temporary employment for two hundred people. This work was desperately needed on the impoverished Reservation.

Pat was more than an inspiration; she was a model of bringing assistance to the Reservation. Sharon Goodhouse said that whenever she was in need, Pat would create a job for her. Sharon took care of Pat's dogs and other matters during Pat's many travels. But what she remembered most was how Pat would tell her about what happened on her trips. She never made anyone feel inadequate. When someone did not understand something, she would just repeat it in such a way that anyone could understand.

Sharon said she never heard Pat put anyone down or say a bad word about anyone. There was one former friend who turned against Pat when she received the MacArthur award. Sharon reported that Pat never fought back. She would just tell Sharon, "You need to stay away from people like that."

She was free with encouragement and good advice. Sharon said, "When I would go through bad times, I would call and she always had good advice. She told me, 'On Saturday take all the bad thoughts in your mind. Put them in a little red wagon. At the end of the week pull it out of your mind and just dump it.'"[60]

Imogene and Dolores Taken Alive had both been invited to take part in the *becoming a woman* ceremony for Pat's granddaughters. They independently commented on the care and thoroughness Pat put into the preparation for this important ceremony.

Deborah Tiger had long been a great admirer of Pat's, to the extent that she asked Pat to be the matron of honor at her wedding.

Even when Deborah had six children, Pat encouraged her to go back to school. Because Deborah suffered from arthritis she had to leave nursing. Instead, she worked in the post office, but she still has plans for further education because she still feels her dear friend's encouragement.

When Pat died, Deborah was determined, despite ill health and little money, to go from the Standing Rock Reservation to Phoenix, Arizona for the funeral. She had her brother-in-law drive her because no one else was available.[61]

The relationship with Frances Makepeace was described in Chapter IV, and that relationship continued, despite Pat's many moves. Frances is not an Indian, but Pat invited her to a sun dance. Frances still goes nearly every year, and she talked about one of the last ones that Pat attended: "She broke her hip and would walk around with a cane. Even at the sun dance, she would walk around the camp and greet everyone, even with her cane. I was in a wheelchair and when it came time to go up to the pole,* she would still dance, pushing me in my wheelchair all the way.

"The last time I saw Pat was at the sun dance. She was a little slower walking, but her beautiful bright spirit was still there. She had these wonderful lessons for people without lecturing or anything. One year there was a girl who had really, really short shorts and was sort of slipping around. She was so obnoxious. Then Pat, in her own way, just talked to her very nicely about modesty, and the girl changed her behavior. Later, the young girl came around and was dancing differently. Pat had done this without hurting feelings or tearing her down or anything. She just talked to her about modesty."[62]

Frances went on to describe how Pat always looked at the bright side of things. One time at a sun dance there were only seven dancers, and rather than being disappointed, Pat was so excited that there were seven dancers. Frances described Pat as a beautiful tapestry that you can't take apart. She was complex and all her activities were interwoven.

---

* About midway through the Lakota sun dance the dancers escort non-dancers to the ceremonial pole in the middle of the dancing area, sometimes refered to as the "tree of life."

Frances's son, Sean, remembers her as a strong Native woman with long black hair. He said, "She was like another mother to me in California." He said that when he saw her for the first time after a long absence, "It was like being reunited with family. She was sort of a mother figure, but also a teacher about Lakota ways and Bahá'í ways. She was a great storyteller." He said she was the kind of person who, when she spoke, people would listen. He went on to say, "She taught me to think before I speak—it goes with wisdom. She helped me become a better listener."[63]

No matter what else she was doing; no matter where she was in various parts of the world; no matter the urgency of the issues on which she was working; no matter the importance of people she might be working with, it was her family, her friends, and her neighbors that remained a constant joy in her heart and to whom she loved to return.

XI

Tȟawáčhiŋ Wašté Wíŋ: Compassionate Woman[64]

Pat was forty-one years old in 1969 when it was decided she should have an Indian name. She was not living on the Reservation, but had been involved with many projects for the benefit of Native people, especially in the field of education. Because she embodied the four virtues most prized by the Lakota—generosity, bravery, respect, and wisdom—it was felt timely to bestow upon her an Indian name reflecting the Lakota woman she had become.

In many places in the world a newborn baby is not given a name. Sometimes this is because infant mortality is so high that naming is put off until it is certain that the child will live. In many eastern cultures a day known as "fête day," usually about six months after the child's birth, is selected as the time to give the child a name. It is often a time of great ceremony.

Before the coming of European settlers, many American Indian tribes waited to see what a child was like. Then a name would be given to reflect some characteristic the child possessed. As the child would grow older a new name might be given to fit the changes in his or her life. Over a person's lifespan he or she might receive several names. For instance, Sitting Bull's first name was *Húŋkešni,* which means *slow, retarded,* or *deliberate.* As a small baby he would pick up objects and seemingly analyze every aspect of them. He was also speech delayed and didn't walk until later than most children usually do. The name was descriptive, not mocking. He also had the name Hoka-Psice (H̄oká Psíče), meaning *Jumping Badger,* which was known to be a temporary name. His father's name was Sitting Bull. After notable feats in a battle with Crow Indians around 1844, when he was about fourteen years old, the young man earned a white eagle feather. At a naming ceremony his father bestowed upon him his own name and the father took the name *Jumping Bull.* At the same time, his father presented the young Sitting Bull with his personalized shield. Today the Lakota use the European method of naming a child at birth.* The birth name fulfills the requirement of identification for a birth certificate, but an Indian name, when given at all, is given later and is highly prized.

In the Lakota sense, one's name is more than a means of identification, a great honor, or even a worthy reward. It has spiritual significance. A highly respected elder will be the one to find an appropriate name. Whoever is to give the name will go into seclusion for several days, often fasting and praying ardently for guidance to find the right name. The elder arrives at the name through inspiration or intuition. It is not a thought process. It takes time for the inspiration to come. When the giver of the name is satisfied that a proper name has been discovered, he returns to his people. When he returns, people know a name has been found even though it is not disclosed yet.

A date and location with spiritual significance are picked for the ceremony. Among the Lakota, a handmade star quilt is prepared for this important event. The star in the quilt represents the morning star that is thought of as a symbol of hope. It shines during the darkest hour before the dawn as a promise of the day to come. It also

---

* It was just a few hundred years ago that Europeans started using surnames as a means of identification for tax purposes. See *Dictionary of Surnames* by Patrick Hanks and Flavia Hodges.

represents the assurance that the covenant that God has made will be fulfilled, that everything dark will be illumined. It is the transition from a bleak, dark, and dreary world into a better one filled with light. It is the symbol of regeneration, the promise of the future. In the name giving ceremony, greater illumination is granted to the one receiving the name, and through that person, to the tribe.

When the group reaches the appropriate spot, the one being given the name steps on the star quilt and remains there throughout the ceremony. The one who came up with the name turns the one receiving it to face each of the four sacred directions. As the honored one faces each direction, the giver of the name announces it. This is also a humble entreaty or prayer begging that the one named will be welcomed and recognized in the hoop of life. From that day forward all creation knows the identity of the one receiving the honor and can call the person by her or his proper name.

In addition to reflecting something of the character of the person, the name serves as a protection and a shield. The one so honored is expected to live up to that name. In so doing, the qualities that were identified are increased and strengthened, providing even greater protection and stability to the individual and, through the one so named, to the entire community. The name may be one someone else has had. More than a nice tribute, it shows a strong similarity and spiritual connection between the two, that the new one reflects qualities of the former. People have confided with conspicuous joy that their Indian name is the one of a beloved ancestor or other relative.

The naming ceremony is also a symbolic journey and prelude to the spirit world. According to at least one commentary on Lakota traditions, when someone dies to this world, he or she reaches a crossroads in the Milkyway, like a fork in the path. There is a gate-keeper called Hinhan Kaga (Hiŋháŋ Káǧa), which literally means "owl-maker," who asks: "Who are you? What is your name?" The person is to give her or his Indian name and, depending on how well the individual lived up to it, he or she will either be allowed to proceed into the spiritual worlds or will have to turn off the straight path and go along the path that leads to nothing. Some people have related this to the legendary role of St. Peter at the pearly gates. One significant difference is that instead of a hellfire of damnation, the other path leads to oblivion. It has also been compared to the Islamic bridge of Sirat.

In the Lakota tradition, loved ones of the departed have a sacred obligation for one year after death. A lock of hair is taken from the deceased person. A family member keeps it in a red cloth. During the year good deeds and services are performed in the name of the one who passed on so that the Hinhan Kaga may find favor with her or him and the forward journey can continue.

At the end of the year, in a special ceremony, the red cloth is taken out and the lock of hair is burned. This is a Lakota sacred rite called "Release of the Soul." The rising smoke represents the release of the departed one's soul to the spirit world. The time allotted for grieving is over and the departed one is now free to go on to the spiritual destiny determined by how well the potential in the name was fulfilled. The Indian name is much more than just a means of identification. It is fundamental both to the person's character and journey in both the temporal world and worlds of the spirit.

For Pat, it was Amos Dog Eagle who had the responsibility of finding her proper name. After several days of prayer and meditation, he knew that her name was to be Tȟawáčhiŋ Wašté Wíŋ, which has been translated variously as "Good-hearted woman," "She has a good consciousness," or "Compassionate woman."

While Pat said many times how honored she felt by this signal event in her life, living up to her name was not always easy. The work she was doing was prone to controversy, setbacks, reversals, and defeats. In moments of unexpected and severe opposition to something she held dear and knew in her heart was right for her people, her natural reaction would be anger and a thirst for revenge. She would have to remind herself of her name and try hard to fulfill it. Instead of taking the natural route of being spurred on by the anger to seek revenge or retaliation, she had the responsibility of finding a compassionate way to deal with the situation. At times she found it a most difficult challenge. Taking the more difficult approach reflected in her name turned out to be a benefit, as it kept serious problems from growing.

Kevin Locke has given a lot of thought to the importance of names.* In many parts of the world, surnames have historically been based on the head of the household's work, where the family lived, or a relationship—such as baker or smith; the prefixes *Mac, O',* or *von;* or the suffixes *son* or *zadeh.* In the modern Western world, family names are passed from one generation to another with, at best, an historical rather than current meaning. Given names are usually a preference of the parents rather than a characteristic of the child. This serves well for the purpose of identification, but modern names are not descriptive. Nicknames, sometimes given later in life, may fill that role.

But in Kevin's view, names should also have a spiritual significance. In his judgment, this is what Hinhan Kaga is seeking after a person dies and he or she is asked, "What is your name?" It is not just asking for a label, but the essence of the individual.† In this view, his mother's name was her path and destiny for both the world of mortals and of the spirit. By right living she would be recognized and called by that name in all the realms beyond this temporal world as she entered a new and wondrous world of illumination. By all accounts, Tȟawáčhiŋ Wašté Wíŋ lived up to her name.

---

* Kevin's Indian name is Tȟokáheya Inážiŋ, which means "The First to Arise." It represents both the first one to serve others in time of need and a standardbearer or one who leads the way.

† In the Biblical story of creation, one of the first tasks given to mankind was to name the creatures of the world. Beyond identification, both custodial and spiritual significance can be inferred from this story.

XII

The Mobridge Tribune

Larry Atkinson, the owner, publisher, and editor of the *Mobridge Tribune*, a local, weekly paper, said that he wanted Pat to help bridge the gap between the two sides of Lake Oahe. He said, "I met Pat a few times at some meetings and was extremely impressed by her intellect, her knowledge, and her ability to understand both the white and Native cultures and walk between the two. She had the ability to explain to non-Natives aspects of the Native culture that they didn't understand that could cause some problems."[65]

He was concerned about racial tensions and explained, "We are a border town. We have many people who don't know very much about their neighbors across the river and don't seem to care to know a lot about them. It leads to racial issues and problems when people do not understand each other, by not understanding where the two cultures are similar and different. This is why racial issues arise."

There needed to be a bridge—not just over the river, but between the two cultures. He wanted Pat to write some articles about Lakota life for the *Mobridge Tribune*. When he approached her, she hesitated. She appreciated the importance of the project, but she was already heavily committed with her own priorities—cultural and language preservation, education, Indian rights, women's rights, the environment, and above all, her family. She had little time or interest in another challenge. Then one day Pat's granddaughter came home from her mostly white elementary school in Mobridge asking what a whore was. When asked where she heard that word, she said her teacher had said that Indians were whores.

That type of language from an educator, and directed at her grandchildren, was too much for Pat. She agreed to write the articles for the paper and focused the energy born of this calloused comment on illumination rather than recrimination. Over the next several years, starting in March of 1987, she wrote more than forty articles. Larry told Pat that he would like one every week, but he knew that would not be possible with her extensive travel and commitments, but he would take whatever she wrote.

So, along with everything else she was doing, she launched into writing articles. While the purpose was to explain Lakota views, they were more than that. These articles capsulate and define much of Pat's thinking. They are a timeless legacy describing her worldview.

Her articles, especially the early ones, were straightforward and positive. She knew how to build bridges of understanding. The issues were sensitive, but she refrained from being confrontational. She gave information and provided insights highlighting what would unite rather than divide. Her first article was carefully crafted and set the tone. Her first two words spoke of family, so important to traditional Lakota as well as whites, followed by a known and positive element—the reputation of her son who was an internationally acclaimed hoop dancer and highly respected by both whites and Indians.*

She started her series by saying, "My son Kevin was invited to teach Lakota culture (at a local elementary school). . . . At the conclu-

---

* The Montana Dakota Utilities Company placed a full-sized roadside billboard with a picture of Kevin dancing and boasted of him as a member of the Montana Dakota Utilities Co. Kevin claims he is an educator who uses dance as his medium, and not a "hoop dancer." He prefers to call his presentation a participatory affirmation and celebration of the oneness of humankind through storytelling, music, and dance. The hoop dances he does are just a small part of his performance.

sion of the classes he performed an intricate dance with twenty-eight hoops and told the students about the significance of the dance."* The hoop dance is a form of prayer used by many Indian tribes since ancient times. Originally, the hoops were wooden limbs that had been soaked to make them soft and pliable to be shaped into hoops. The hoop represents the circle of life because the circle is one of the most common geometric forms in the world. It is basic to all creation. Therefore, the hoop represents a sign of the Creator in all things. It also illustrates the principles of unity, renewal, and spiritual rebirth. It is found everywhere with limitless symbolic meanings. The hoop dance, then, is a prayer paying homage to both Creation and to the Creator.

She went on to explain, "To the Lakota people, the hoop is symbolic of the circle of life. Another term is the sacred hoop.

"On the prairie here, we live within that sacred hoop of life. If we stand on any hill, and if we turn 360 degrees around, we can see on the horizon this circle or hoop where the sky meets the earth. The awesomeness of the Creator's work is evident."

Pat loved the natural beauty on the Reservation and had been heard to complain that when she would spend too much time in urban areas she would suffer from what she called "horizon deprivation."

The article went on to explain that by using different colored hoops, Kevin would form a globe symbolizing that the world was made of interconnected people of all races and all things of the earth. He would then pull out one hoop and the whole thing would collapse, demonstrating our interdependencies. Pat made her point of essential oneness before touching on the issue of local disharmony. Then, in a gentle way, she mentioned local problems by saying, "While our degree of disharmony is minimal compared to that suffered by other racial conflicts around the world, I know

---

* See Kevin's Web Site for more information: http://www.kevinlocke.com/kevin/index.html.

that even this minimal degree is the cause of pain among our children of both races.

"I'm convinced that the disharmony arises because we lack understanding of one another."

She concluded her first article by saying, "We don't quite understand so many aspects of our differing cultures—the different but still valid ways we worship God, our value systems, our male / female behavior expectations, our political status, our perspectives of history, and even such basic concepts as a worldview.

"In the coming weeks and months I will talk about the Lakota perspective of these beliefs, behaviors and concepts. I know that some of this information will be redundant to many because nearly every day I'm made aware of the generosity of heart that is extended to my family by Indian and white alike.

"I hope this column will fill the gaps of understanding that still exist in our community. I believe that together we can strengthen our intertwining circle of life."[66]

In a later article she used a funeral to explain some fundamental Lakota values: the spiritual nature of children; the "give away," which is a means of saying that relationships and friendship are more important than material things; that help should be given to one another; and that special respect and regard should be given for elders. In a subtle way it also suggests that true wealth is what you share, not what you keep.

Her next article pointed out some specific cultural differences. Indian children are taught that it is rude and aggressive to stare directly into another person's eyes, whereas white children are taught to maintain eye contact while talking and that not doing so suggests dishonesty and rudeness. For the Lakota a handshake, when done at all, is short and gentle, instead of the firm grip and hearty shake that is taken as a sign of sincerity among whites. The typical distance between whites in conversation is about eight inches, while the Lakota prefer about a forty-inch gap.* The final thing mentioned was

---

* This varies from tribe to tribe.

that adults should touch a child only with love. The mere thought of corporeal punishment is horrifying, especially in public schools.

She reported on a recent survey in South Dakota that mentioned the many misperceptions people had about Indians, their way of life, and their relationship with the federal government. Other articles mentioned efforts to counter alcoholism on the Reservation as well as other common concerns such as the status of teachers, bravehearted women, and parenting. She wrote of some outstanding contemporary Indian women to illustrate the fundamental notion of respect for elders. She wrote an article suggesting five books for greater understanding.*

In her article on "Bravehearted women" she pointed out that among the Lakota the equality of men and women was an established fact. They had long lived the objectives of the then-prominent women's movement. She spoke of the special group who would see to the protection of the camp when the men were out hunting, or wait on horseback at the edge of battle to retrieve and tend to the wounded. The story of the girl who saved her brother was mentioned earlier. She explained: "There are still bravehearted women today. They serve the people as lobbyists, attorneys, physicians, nurses, educators, judges, and advocates in many less spectacular roles."[67] It is worth repeating that she included among the bravehearted women of today the mothers raising their children in impoverished circumstances with insufficient funds, inadequate housing, and little hope for relief.

Her next article was not restricted to Indian issues, but dealt with education in general. She lamented the fact that South Dakota teachers were at the bottom of the pay scale in the United States and stressed the importance of the profession.

---

* The five books are: Vine Deloria, Jr. (ed.), *American Indian Policy in the Twentieth Century.* Norman, OK: University of Oklahoma Press, 1985; Peter Matthiessen, *Indian Country.* New York: The Viking Press, 1984; Francis Paul Prucha, *American Indian Policy in the Formative Years.* Lincoln, NE: University of Nebraska Press, 1973; Evan S. Connell, *Sun of the Morning Star.* San Francisco: North Point Press, 1984; and Sam D. Gill, *Native American Traditions.* Belmont, CA: Wadsworth Publishing Co., 1983.

She wrote about parenting, focusing on old ways of raising children, which were gentle, involved the extended family, and included the entire village. This was wiped away when children were forcibly taken to boarding schools or placed in foster home care where, at times, physical punishment was used, even to the point of causing injury to young Indian children.

She wrote of the misunderstandings caused by what is termed "wait-time." That is, rather than a quick response to comments or questions, especially of a personal nature, there is a tendency in the Lakota culture to pause, sometimes for days, in reflecting on the proper response. Many non-Indians think of this as being slow witted. Rather, it is a deep and thorough consideration of what is honored as an important question worth a serious answer.

She reported on a major event on the Reservation in which over 1,400 people ran in support of sobriety, admitting that she didn't run the full distance. She did quite a sprint but quit when she saw the business end of a snake threatening her.

In an article supporting the teaching of Lakota on the Reservation schools, she pointed out that language is a window to the world and studies have shown that youngsters proficient in more than one language are ahead of those who can use only one. She lamented the law that mandated that English be the only spoken language in the schools.

One reader wrote, "I've lived near Indian people for more than 40 years and some of the things she has written are new to me. Thank you, Pat and thank you Tribune, for enriching our knowledge and making us look forward more than ever to reading the Tribune. . . ."[68]

It wasn't until after building a firm foundation of understanding that she began to write about more controversial issues. On May 12, 1987 she spoke of the solidarity of eight Indian tribes supporting the Oglala Sioux, who were appealing injustices. A month later, on June 7, 1987, she wrote about the centennial of the United States Constitution and how strange it was that the media coverage she saw made no mention of Indians. She pointed out seven specific references to Indians in the Constitution and explained that the constitutional systems set up by a number of eastern tribes, especially from the Iroquois Confederacy, formed much of the basic framework of the U.S. Constitution. It is worth noting that the Iroquois Confederacy was formed around 1560, more than 200 years before the U.S. Constitution was drafted. Early European settlers marveled at the degree of personal freedom individuals had under the confederacy.

When Secretary of War John Jay gave out instructions for the Continental Convention in 1787, the instructions included the statement: "The United States are fixed in their determination that justice and public faith will be the basis of all transactions with the Indians. They will reject every advantage obtained at the expense of these important national principles."[69]

Pat refrained from pointing out how often that basic direction had been ignored. Considering the indignities heaped upon her people in general and her relatives in particular, a strident, militant, confrontational response would not be surprising, but she chose to frame the issue in a neutral, evenhanded way. She used this moderate approach despite the fact that President Lincoln had signed the executive order for the hanging of thirty-eight of her Dakota relatives; her great-grandfather, Little Crow, had been shot and killed for his scalp; and her grandfather, Noel, had to flee from Minnesota so fast he was called "Flying Earth" in his escape from persecution. She and her family members had endured indignities that could not be changed, but her writing remained positive and she focused her energy on issues that could be improved.

On the way to expressing more controversial views, she wrote about one of the many common affronts that people make unthinkingly. The example she used was the name for a boat ramp for a recreational area. The Army Corps of Engineers named it the "Indian Memorial" boat ramp. Pat pointed out that the word "memorial" is used for dead people. The implication is that Indians no longer existed—they were a thing of the past. She felt it would be more appropriate to single out an Indian no longer living, such as Sitting Bull, for the honor of having a memorial. Indians, as a group, were still very much alive. She used that example to point out the countless slights that Indians face every day, often from thoughtlessness rather than malice.

Then she set aside her low-key approach. On February 10, 1988, a year after she started the series and within two days of the anniversary of Lincoln's birthday, she wrote her most controversial piece. It was at a time when there was a great clamor in the United States to insist that South Africa give up its policy of Apartheid. There were demonstrations demanding a boycott of South African goods because of this repressive policy. All the shouting and demonstrations made no reference to America's apartheid history.

Pat wrote an article titled "Apartheid has nothing on Lincoln." She wrote of the brutal atrocities that were the official policies of the Lincoln administration for the annihilation of any and all Indians who would not assimilate. The policy of the Lincoln administration was "to kill as many Indians as possible." This reflected the nineteenth-century European mindset that non-European and non-Christian people were less than human and therefore available for exploitation. Their property and other items could be taken with impunity. Some Europeans even considered it a sacred duty either to convert or subdue non-Christians. Atrocious violence was unleashed against Midwestern Indians—Dakota, Lakota, Nez Percé, Cheyenne, Ute, Navajo, Apache, Winnebago, Arapaho, Chippewa, and others—who were obstacles to western expansion. Kit Carson, a western gunman and noted "Indian killer," was ordered to "lay waste the prairies by fire (and to) kill all Apache men whenever and wherever you find them."[70]

In general the Indians were considered savages who interfered with the westward expansion of the nation. They were not considered Americans; they were the enemy! Many even believed Indians to be subhuman. Any and all measures needed to continue the expansion of the American nation were thought appropriate. Clearly the attitude was that of being at war with the Indians, and "Indian fighters" (those who fought against and killed Indians) were highly regarded and were considered the heroes of the day. There was no Geneva Convention, nor any other kind of restraint.

In his address to Congress in 1863, Lincoln "expressed pride concerning the removal of many tribes, 'sundry treaties' and 'extinguishing the possessory rights of the Indians to large and valuable tracts of land.'" Mention of the acquisition of Indian land was consistent with Lincoln's professional life. Before becoming president, he was a corporate lawyer for railroad interests during the time of their westward expansion. Indian land interfered with expansionary goals.

To Pat, this carnage was personal. The thirty-eight Dakota who were hanged by Lincoln's decree were her relatives. Lincoln also sanctioned the incarceration of another 1,600 men, women, and children in Fort Snelling in what is now known as Minnesota. She concluded the article by saying that for her, Lincoln's birthday was a day of mourning. On that day she would gather her children and grandchildren to say prayers for the departed souls of Lincoln's victims as well as "for the soul of Abraham Lincoln."[71]

When she sent her grandchildren to school on Lincoln's birthday, she had them wear black armbands in mourning. The teacher asked their mother, Pat's daughter Winona Flying Earth, why the children were wearing the black armbands. When Winona explained the reason, she was told that the next year the children could be excused from school on that day.

In the article she also mentioned that Mount Rushmore was sacred ground for Indians and that she considered Lincoln's likeness there to be a blasphemy. Some Indians have considered the replacement of the Indian-head penny with the Lincoln-head penny as a metaphor for the repression and planned annihilation experienced under him and that his image on Mount Rushmore was the ultimate insult.

Atkinson confided that that was his favorite article. He said it was an eye-opener and stimulated more discussion in the community than any of the others. It gave people information that is generally neglected in classes on American history.

In another article, called "Unlocking Education," she spoke of the kind of education that has nothing to do with book learning. She described the education she received from her parents. She said, "My father taught me as a baby to expect miracles. I knew and know that miracles are commonplace."[72] She went on to describe watching her father make rain when it was needed and stopping it when there was enough. The ability to accept and acknowledge the unbelievable became the foundation of her education. She illustrated that the most significant education begins at home. She was unlocking ideas far beyond what is learned in school.

In January of 1989 she wrote an article called the "Barbados Declaration." A declaration had been put together by the Symposium of Inter-Ethnic Conflict in South America, sponsored by the World Council of Churches, in 1971. This declaration detailed many of the atrocities against indigenous people throughout the Americas. It included a call for action on the part of governments, and listed ten specific steps to be taken. She quoted an anthropologist who said it was the responsibility of the scientific community to ". . . denounce systematically by any and all means cases of genocide and those practices conducive to ethnocide; and finally, the responsibility of Indians as agents of their own destiny."[73] The vigor of this article reflected her own stunning blow from the Supreme Court decision denying the practice of Indian religions as discussed in Chapter VII.

Several months later she wrote about something closer to home. An article, bearing the caption "More than 900 run for sobriety," told of an annual running event to highlight the need to combat rampant alcoholism. Each runner carried a prayer stick, a long pole adorned with eagle feathers, and a red cloth tobacco tie at the top. Red cloth is used to hold the tobacco for the sacred pipe smoked in the sweat ceremony. She explained, "These prayer sticks represented the hopes and prayers of all the people at Standing Rock that soon the Lakota and Dakota will regain total sobriety."[74] A stick for the occasion was sent by inmates from the State Penitentiary in North Dakota, and some Indians on deathrow at San Quentin learned of the run and had some eagle feathers sent to the North Dakota inmates to show their support.

Her January 31, 1990 article spoke of her participation, together with two of her granddaughters, Maymangwa Flying Earth-Miranda and Kimimila Locke, in the Martin Luther King, Jr. celebration in

Atlanta. The common concerns of Indians and African Americans were touched on, as well as the progress both groups have made in the hard-fought struggle for their respective rights and dignity. As a reflection of her inherent modesty, she did not mention the close relationship she had with Coretta Scott King. At other times Pat has spoken of the support and guidance she has gotten from discussing issues with Mrs. King, especially about getting appropriate action from the government.

In an article a month later she lamented the fact that her own education called attention to the Greek traditions and the Magna Carta as foundations of democracy. Little mention had been made of the fact that American democracy, emphasizing the rights of individuals, is more of a legacy from American Indian customs than of European origin. Citing Jack Wetherford's book, *Indian Givers: How the Indians of America transformed the world*,[75] she described how "The people from the Old World were amazed at the Indian's personal liberty and their freedom from rulers and from social classes based on ownership of property."[76] She then mentioned the impact the Iroquois Confederacy had on such founders of American democracy as Benjamin Franklin, Thomas Jefferson, and Thomas Paine in their efforts to form a more equitable society. Jefferson was greatly impressed by the advanced thinking for governance found in the Iroquois Confederacy. However, when he realized that the Indians, as a group, would not assimilate into the European styled culture, he lost interest in them. She specifically mentioned the impact of the writers Sir Thomas Moore—who popularized the Greek word *utopia,* meaning *ideal state*—and Michael de Montaigne in spreading ". . . the word that Indians lived in a more just, equitable, and egalitarian society than did Europeans."

In subsequent articles she went back to Lakota traditions, describing the sacredness of the Lakota pipe. It was a symbol of the covenant with the Creator and is used in Lakota sacred rites. Commercialization of cultural items distressed her greatly. Other Indians are also disturbed by commercialization of what they hold dear and sacred. They refer to this as "selling the culture." Among the items that many think should not be commercialized are selling replicas of the sacred pipe as souvenirs and performing dances for money and entertainment for non-Indian audiences. These are both considered forms of commercialization, found contemptible by many Indians.* Pat went on to speak of the significance of the powwow and how people will sacrifice a great deal to attend and for their success.

The importance of generosity and compassion for a Lakota was the subject of another article. She said, "The best that can be said of anyone would be such observations as: 'She is always friendly and willing to give her time . . . she will help you out in a pinch . . . she'll give you a ride . . . she'll listen to you when you've got troubles . . . she has a big heart.'"[77] She also pointed out the importance of the give-away. She said, "Most Lakota homes have a trunk or boxes where future give-away objects are collected or stored . . . time is spent making shawls, beaded goods, quilts, and other objects for the future give-aways. . . ."[78] This is an expression of the Lakota belief that true wealth lies in what one shares, not what is accumulated.

An article in May of that year pointed out that children (wakan yeja or sacred beings) have historically been considered holy gifts from God to be treated lovingly and with respect. Then she expressed grief that, ". . . in today's world as Indians increasingly accept the values and behaviors of the white society, the abuse of children and family violence have become as prevalent in the Indian world as it is in the white world."[79] In an attempt to counteract this, she described a march held on the Reservation protesting violence against children.

She said it has been estimated that before Columbus's voyages, between ninety and one hundred million Indians inhabited North America. By 1900 the United States census listed fewer than 300,000

---

* There is an important difference between the commercialized dancing for the entertainment of non-Indian audiences and what Kevin does. Kevin dances as an educational device, explaining the sacred aspects of his various dances. With this he demonstrates the oneness and interconnectedness of all mankind. He considers himself a teacher using dance as his medium. Hoop dances are just a part of his presentation.

Indians and the current estimate is around one million. She maintained that bravery enabled the remaining ones to survive in the face of incredible obstacles.

Both the difficulty and importance of seeking wisdom have been subjects of her articles. She quoted Pete Catches as saying, "Life is like a huge design. Each part of the design is made up of the happening, acts and interactions of people with each other and the world. You must know that this design is completed by the intervention of Wakan Tanka (Wakȟáŋ Tȟáŋka). This term is used in different ways. It can refer to either the Creator or Creation, depending on context. It can also mean that all aspects of creation are indivisible parts of the spiritual world. It does not imply pantheism.

"People and this world and all that is in it are only a part of Wakan Tanka. . . . Yet from the holy goodness of Wakan Tanka a way was given . . . that we may pray and have a glimpse, a little knowledge, of the Great Mystery that is life."[80]

She stressed that for a Lakota, knowing the language is part of gaining an appreciation for the interrelatedness of the wind and weather and all parts of creation, because these concepts are intertwined with the language. This includes learning the significance of the four sacred colors—red, yellow, black, and white—as representing the fundamental oneness of mankind. One aspect of the Lakota language and culture, so at odds with the prevailing American culture, especially found in humor and politics, is that language should not be used to say anything bad about another person.

She went on to quote Pete Catches as saying, "The world was a library and its books were the stones, leaves, grass, brooks and the birds and animals that shared, alike with us, the storms and blessings of earth. We learned to do what only the student of nature ever learns, and that was to feel beauty. We never railed at the storms, the furious winds and the biting frosts and snows. . . . We sit in the lap of our Mother. From her we, and all other livings things, come. We shall soon pass, but the place where we now rest will last forever."[81]

In November of 1990 Pat joyously announced the signing into law of the Native American Language Act. For 104 years the use of Native languages in schools had been illegal.[82] The congressional Executive Document of 1886 banning the use of Native languages in schools stated: ". . . no books in any Indian language must be used or instructions given in that language . . . the rule will be strictly enforced." The Native American Language Act of 1990 finally reversed this and made it legal for the first time in over a hundred years for Indian children to use their mother tongue—the language of the heart—in school. With all the work Pat had done, at the very forefront of working for the right to use Native languages in schools, it is easy to imagine her personal satisfaction.

Several key elements stand out in her November 28, 1990 article on the Lakota view of the child. Among them is the view of the child as a sacred being. Before birth the spirit of the child selects the family in which it is to be raised; much holding, touching, and hugging is essential to babies, including singing, talking, and massaging the child in utero; playfulness and joyfulness are expressed while discipline is to be gentle. Kindness to others is also stressed. She mentioned two kinds of education among the Lakota: "Kaonspe (Kaúŋspe or Kaúŋspepi), education by force as in breaking a horse, and Woksapa (Wóksapa), a broadly conceived adjustment to nature and all its aspects. . . ."[83] She concluded the article by saying, ". . . all the adults in a community are responsible for the safety and happiness of the collective wakan yeja. The effect of this love on the children is a feeling of security and self assurance. Children are put first in all things."[84]

There had been an article in the *Mobridge Tribune* that had derogatory remarks about Sitting Bull. The article was submitted by the trustees of the Over Indian Museum of the University of South Dakota citing an account by William H. Over, which Pat considered "seriously flawed." In her article of December 12, 1990 she voiced strong indignation over that account. Throughout her life, Pat was indignant over misleading comments by so-called scholars about Indians and Indian ways. It concerned her that these statements often become accepted as fact when, in reality, they are but one person's distorted or incomplete understanding.

Her final article traced the history of Indian sovereignty issues. She pointed out that the Constitution decrees that "treaties are the supreme law of the land." Yet, among the 370 signed treaties with various Indian nations, many have been disregarded or ignored in violation of that constitutional provision. Treaties that interfered with other objectives were trammeled upon with little consideration as to what was either legal or right.

A classic example of selective enforcement involved the Cherokee nation. In 1831 the U.S. Supreme Court ruled in favor of protecting Cherokee land in Georgia. The state wanted prospectors to look for gold in the Indian region. The Supreme Court said the state had no authority there. President Andrew Jackson was reputed to have said: "John Marshall (the Chief Justice) . . . has made his decision; now let him enforce it!" There is no record that Jackson actually made that oft-quoted remark, but it reflects the attitude of the day, and the ruling was not enforced. In contrast, the Indian Removal Act of 1830, which passed by only one vote, was strictly enforced. It became the basis for the violation of a multitude of previous treaties. One result was the "Trail of Tears" in 1838 in which 17,000 Cherokee were removed from the land specifically protected in the Supreme Court ruling of 1831 and forced to march to Indian Territory in present-day Oklahoma. It was a bitterly cold winter and they had inadequate provisions. Nearly one out of four Cherokee—more than 4,000 people— perished along the way.

Pat spoke of the need for continued diligence to make sure legal treaties are enforced. Her final paragraph reads: "Next year, in 1992, many Indian Nations will be celebrating their survival of the past 500 years (since Columbus's voyages). It would be appropriate that our guests (people of non-Indian descent) help us to retain and regain our dignity and human rights."[85]

While not mentioned in that article, she pointed out in a talk at the University of Southern Maine that Felix S. Cohen wrote a handbook on American Indian law. It consists of 4,200 often conflicting federal laws. He said Indians are like the miners' canary. When bad things are about to happen in America, it happens to the Indians first because they are the weakest and least powerful.

Larry Atkins, the owner and publisher of the *Mobridge Tribune*, was so right to lament the fact that no more prose would be published from the pen of Pat.

XIII

Bolivia and Peru [86]

Many of the articles Pat wrote for the *Mobridge Tribune* were covered in Chapter XII. Reporting on her trip to Bolivia and Peru was different. None of the other articles were about her. When one of her trips was mentioned at all, it was incidental to whatever else she was trying to say. This was not the case with the three articles she wrote about her trip to Peru and Bolivia. The trip was the focus and she was the main character. While most other topics were discussed within one article, she wrote three articles about this particular trip. The other articles explained Lakota life and beliefs; reported important events on the Reservation; spoke out on specific injustices; or encouraged high value issues such as education, the sacred nature of children, or the rights of women. These three articles were about her!

Her getting to Bolivia is a story in itself. She and Kevin traveled together to many parts of the world, but always worked independently. Pat, the activist, would be involved with indigenous and government leaders dealing with issues such as education, language preservation, rights of indigenous people, women's rights, the environment, and other matters. Kevin, the educator, used his dance routines to promote the idea of the oneness of mankind and to illustrate the interrelatedness of all creation. They each honored, respected, and were supportive of the work of the other. While freely discussing what they were doing, neither entered directly into the other's activities. They traveled together because they enjoyed each other's company.

Kevin had become a Bahá'í in 1979.[87] But Pat had not enrolled. The Bahá'í Faith is a world religion that upholds that all religions come from the same source. According to the teachings of the Faith, every 500 to 1,000 years a divine teacher is sent to humanity bringing the teachings most urgent for a particular time and place. Among Them are Krishna, Zoroaster, Moses, Buddha, Christ, Muhammad, and, most recently, Bahá'u'lláh. A Bahá'í is someone who recognizes Bahá'u'lláh as the Messenger from God for this age. Among His teaching are: the essential unity of all religions, the equality of men and women, elimination of prejudice, that the earth should be regarded as one country, and that the time is at hand for peace to be established throughout the world.

In 1988 Kevin was asked to participate in a Bahá'í program of exchange in which Native American Bahá'ís from North America would travel to South America. In like manner, Indian Bahá'ís from South America have traveled to North America to dance for one another. This exchange, known as the "Camino del Sol" ("Trail of Light" or "Path of the Sun"), had its origin in 1982 when a group of North American Bahá'í Natives visited South America. In 1983 there was a visit from the south.

In 1988 Kevin was invited to take part in a similar trip. This trip was clearly meant for Indian Bahá'ís of North America to share their dancing and songs with those of the south. Despite this, Kevin took it upon himself to invite his mother to come along even though she was not a Bahá'í. She agreed.

Another Bahá'í, Jacqueline Left Hand Bull, was to be a member of the traveling team. She had met Pat only once, very briefly, but had heard a lot about her. The work she was doing for Indian colleges and cultural preservation was well-known and created a sense of awe. According to Jacqueline, Pat had a reputation as a force to be reckoned with: a strong woman who got things done despite fierce opposition. Jacqueline had also done some work on cultural matters, but feared her efforts would seem puny compared to Pat's. In brief, Jacqueline was afraid of Pat and was terrified when she learned that Kevin had invited his mother on the South American trip. Even though she told Kevin that was nice, she exclaimed to herself: "Oh my God! Three weeks with Pat Locke! I'll be mashed potatoes by the time it's over!"[88] The party that was to travel to South America met in Wakpala, South Dakota, in preparation for the trip. That was the first time Jacqueline spent significant time with Pat. She said, "I could not believe what a kind and thoughtful person she was. I thought I was in the presence of royalty . . . we became the best of friends. We would . . . talk and talk." That was the beginning of a deep and lasting friendship. When they were not together they would call each other several times a week, just to talk. During later trips they would sometimes share a room to save expenses. After making necessary preparations in Wakpala, they were on their way.

When Pat returned, she started writing about her trip for the *Mobridge Tribune*. She called the first article "Dreams come true in Bolivia and Peru." She said: "A few weeks ago a dream came true for me and I walked through the hidden city of the Incas. . . . When we left South Dakota it was late summer. Twenty hours later when we arrived in Santa Cruz, Bolivia, it was early spring and the fruit trees were blossoming pink."

The world looks very different from the two hemispheres. Not only are the seasons reversed; sights, sounds, smells, and even tastes go from the familiar to the strange and exotic. When looking south from the northern temperate zone, the sun courses the sky from left to right. From the south it seems to move from right to left. It is strange to wake up in the morning and see the sun rising on your right. Then, at night, you can watch the sun set to your left. The stars look different too. Not only are there different constellations—you can see only two stars of the Big Dipper, and they are reversed—but there is the Southern Cross. Familiar constellations are reversed when seen from the other perspective. Water going down a drain takes a clockwise path in the north. In the south it is counterclockwise.

The foods were different too. The travelers ate fruit they had never tasted before that had Spanish names such as cherimoya, quanabana, guayaba, jicama, mamoncillo, and tamarindo. At one place they ate grilled llama. Pat could swallow only one bite, remembering the soft, huge eyes of these animals that grazed everywhere on the mountainsides of the Andes. They ate more varieties of potato and corn than they knew existed.

As is common when in strange places, Pat would look up into the night sky for reassurance. But the familiar was not there to reassure. The moon was lying on her back like a cantaloupe slice ready to be eaten. The Big Dipper and the other familiar constellations were gone, replaced by other worlds.

These differences were confusing. Ceremonially, the Lakota always move clockwise. But when they started to dance at a Quechua village, they almost started counterclockwise because they had watched water drain counterclockwise down the bathroom sink and it swirled their thinking.

For Pat, a wonderful part of the dream-like reality was that, for nearly four weeks, they were surrounded by Indians. For her, it was like being in Indian heaven where everyone had dark and shining eyes, brown skin, black and gleaming hair, and a warm, welcoming smile that said, "Ah, here you are, our relatives from the north, we're glad that you're here visiting us again." They recognized their ancestors in the faces of one another.

Language was another major problem. They could not exchange words directly with any of the Quechua or Aymara speaking hosts. There they were: four North American Indians in the midst of seventeen million Quechua and two million Aymara Indians who were speaking their own languages. Fewer than half of the northern visitors even knew a little Spanish, the language many North Americans think everyone in South America speaks. So, even though they knew a little Spanish, they were totally ignorant of the other languages. Fortunately, they had good interpreters.

In her articles she pointed out that these indigenous people, who are the descendants of the victims of the conquistadores, were legally serfs until a 1952 revolution. Everyone they met who was over thirty-four years old had literally been born into slavery.

Most travel books like to describe the Incas of the Andes as abject, mute, or resentful—which is often the way that North American Indians are perceived. Pat found these Incas to be witty, open, warm, and full of joy.

She also pointed out that white travelers face formidable barriers of language and culture. In the world's highest inhabited regions, most tourists see lives lived in barren isolation where the people exist without television, automobiles, telephones, or shopping centers and wonder how they can exist without these artificial necessities. These North Americans saw the people differently. They were lucky enough to travel to places tourists don't go, they had Native translators, and they appreciated the relief they felt from the frenetic North American urban life.

The geography was also unfamiliar. Pat, after all, was from the Great Plains of the temperate zone of the north—far from the tropics. The journey began in the lush tropics with their unfamiliar vegetation. Brilliantly colored flowers were everywhere, perfuming the nostrils of these northern visitors as they walked by.

Santa Cruz, the largest city in Bolivia, was the first South American stop. The group went to Nur University where students were studying computer technology, as well as animal husbandry and horticulture. Afterward Pat wondered why they were studying agriculture when she remembered that the Indians of Central and South America have always been agricultural geniuses, as they had developed eighty-five percent of the food that today feeds the world. She wondered what they, of all people, could learn from books about agriculture. However, she had been too dazzled by the lush tropical surroundings to ask.

Sensual winds embraced them and followed them through the streets of Santa Cruz. They were taken to the outskirts of the city where eighty boys and girls danced, sang, and recited for them. When it came time for the North Americans to perform, the children treated them like rock stars, screaming bloody murder after each one performed. After a few days they took their dancing to nearby populated cities.

They flew to Sucre, the constitutional capital. They were taken to the outskirts of town to a meeting place where about sixty Indians had been waiting for them all day. The people were referred to as *campensinos,* or country people, many of whom had walked two or three days to greet them. It was evening. Each came singly up to each of the visitors, smiled, looked straight into their faces, and touched each with the special Quechua greeting: first, they shake hands. Then they briefly grip one another's shoulders. Finally, they shake hands again, smiling all the while. Pat came to enjoy this greeting, which is so different from her familiar Lakota style in which the hand is held ever so lightly and there is one short hand pump.

Every one of the *campesinos* was dressed in beautiful handwoven garments of the softest alpaca and sheep's wool. The designs were intricate. The colors were glorious. She compared them with her own store-bought, synthetic, and massproduced clothes, which she felt were dull-colored and unimaginatively textured. They seemed pitiful in comparison.

They were also special guests at a wedding. The bride and groom had waited an extra day so the guests from the north could witness their bonding. After the ceremony there were dances and a variety of flutes were played by the local Indians.

From there the group piled into two jeeps to travel on roads—Pat thought of them as trails—to more remote places. Jacqueline said she was terrified of the roads and had she known how they were going to travel, she probably would not have gone. She said, "The road was not flat and there were washouts and you felt the car would turn over. You could look straight down, maybe 3,000 feet and not even see the bottom."

They started with a hair-raising, six-hour ride to a remote Peruvian village called Mayu. Since Pat was the elder of the group, she was given the seat of honor—in front, next to the driver. They traveled through unimaginably high mountain passes and onto a high plain, the Altiplano, in the midst of the Andes. They traveled along the shores of Lake Titicaca, the highest navigable lake in the

A long, narrow, and winding road in Bolivia

world. Locals consider it the birthplace of humankind. Glaciers were commonplace as they moved through the jungles and ruins of the old Incan Empire. At Machu Picchu, they were two-and-a-half miles above sea level. Pat had stopped a forty-four year old habit of smoking two weeks before going so she could breathe the rarified air of high altitudes and not embarrass herself or Kevin climbing the steep stone steps of the Inca sites. She resumed the habit when she got back home.

Felix, the driver, was competent and obviously familiar with the trails. Pat did her best not to disturb him as she braked, flinched, and leaned way over into each curve to prevent their tipping over and falling down the thousand foot chasms. She would throw her head into his lap so she wouldn't have to look ahead. She prided herself in not screaming. Instead she shut her eyes on the worst curves, missing some spectacular scenery. If she saw Kevin looking out the window trying to look down, she would say, "Kevin, don't do that. You'll make us fall." Everyone would laugh, but it was clear she was terrified.

A view of a precipice adjacent to a Bolivian road

In order to not think of the road she would talk about other things. She would say to Jacqueline, "You know I have six grandchildren and here are their names." Then she would go on about what the names meant so she didn't have to look at or think about that road.

It was dark when they arrived at Mayu and they had to hike half a mile up a steep, rocky path in the thin air to get to the adobe home where they spent the night. They were given a delicious soup, tea, and bread before bedding down in sleepingbags spread out on the earthen floor. They were told not to worry about *venchugas*. Venchugas are little beasts that crawl down the walls in the dark and find your eyeballs. There they lay wastes that will cause a lingering death. Pat nearly suffocated in her sleeping bag hiding from the venchugas.

In the morning they ate limes, fresh bread, and tea and washed their faces in the cold mountain stream that flowed by the house. They sat by the stream and watched several teenage girls exchange secrets, dip their fingers in the water, and braid their long black hair.

Then the North Americans changed into their Native regalia and climbed to a threshing circle where some fifty people were gathered. There were two or three dwellings in the distance surrounded by blossoming fruit trees. The mountainsides were steeply terraced. An occasional shepherd boy could be seen perched on a jagged rock formation to listen to the songs that echoed down the valley. It seemed appropriate that when Kevin played Lakota courting songs on his flute, two condors and two eagles soared overhead. North and South American Indians held hands and danced together to Lakota and Quechua songs.

On the treacherous drive back to Sucre, the group decided that Pat should not sit in the terrifying seat of honor with the driver. She was reassigned to the backseat, on the side away from steep drop-offs. It was just as treacherous, but at least she didn't have to see it.

Still in Peru, their next venture was to Misque Pampa. Pat rode all the way in the backseat facing away from the precipices. This was a long, long journey, up hairpin turns to nearly the peak of one mountain, then on to another higher mountain pass, and another, and another, and another. In some places the road seemed only about eight inches wider than the jeep. She bit her upper lip as they passed an oncoming car on this impossibly narrow road. The terrifying ride lasted nine hours, but it seemed an eternity.

A narrow Bolivian road

Felix, the driver, would glance back occasionally to see how far behind the other jeep was. Pat wanted to say, "Keep your eyes on the road, I'll watch for you." But she would just shut her eyes. They would stop once in awhile so people could stretch their legs and break up the long ride. After so many hours in the car they were getting tired and hungry.

After dark the driver cut the lights, rolled down his window, and said, "Listen." While still a few miles from the village, drumming and singing could be heard off in the distance. There were about twenty people wearing white clothing, playing long drums and flutes. When the jeep arrived at the village, the people came and opened the back door and the cramped inhabitants sort of unfolded and spilled out into the night air. About eighty Indians were standing along the side of the road singing a welcome song. The bright full moon illumined everyone.

The villagers then formed a long welcoming line and each one in turn greeted the visitors with the word: "Alláh-u-Abhá." This was a precious and familiar greeting for the Bahá'ís who would answer "Alláh-u-Abhá" in return. This is an Arabic phrase meaning, "God is All-Glorious." It is used by Bahá'ís all over the world as a greeting, and has been used ever since Bahá'u'lláh made His formal declaration as being the Promised One of all ages in Baghdad in 1863. It distinguishes Bahá'ís from Muslims, who use the greeting "Alláh-u-Akbar." For Pat, who was the only member of the team who was not a Bahá'í, it was unfamiliar. She would respond, "Hello, hello" in a friendly, but more formal way. As the greeting line continued she started to respond more warmly that she was happy to meet them. By the time she reached the end of the line she was choking back tears saying, "Alláh-u-Abhá." Jacqueline was right behind her and she knew, at that moment, that Pat had accepted the Faith. She exclaimed to herself, "She's in!"

Pat was incapable of being anything but honest and sincere in anything she said or did. So, by the end of the reception line, when she was saying "Alláh-u-Abhá," she was still meaning "hello" and "I'm happy to meet you," but there was now an added message: "I'm one of you."

From the receiving line, the visitors walked along the moonlit path to the home of Fermin Valleyo, where they would be staying. Fermin and his sister Delores were heroes of the 1952 revolution. They always wear white clothing in honor of those times. That night Pat and the other visitors slept on soft woven blankets laid on the swept earthen floor. A small high window was on one wall. On another wall were clothing pegs and a few tools on higher pegs. On a third wall was a calendar and a large poster commemorating a meeting of indigenous women. Pat admired the austerity of this room and thought of her own cluttered bedroom in South Dakota.

The next day, people from thirteen nearby villages arrived. They had walked to the village to dance with the North American visitors. They danced and sang and visited for hours in another large threshing circle. Pat was slightly dizzy now and then from a lack of oxygen and the intense heat of the sun, but was comforted by a dry breeze. She wanted to take a nap, but resisted because she knew she would never experience anything like this again, so she kept on dancing.

As they were about to leave, a young woman of about thirty was brought to meet them. Her face was strong and beautiful. Her eyes were somehow fierce. They were told she wanted advice. She was known as a most courageous woman of the Misque Pampa because she had defied authorities who were attempting to suppress the indigenous culture, and she wanted advice.

Pat wondered: "What could we say at the last minute? The jeep's motor was running. We could only tell her to be strong and to always think of the children." Pat expressed regret about not being able to speak more with this young woman and share experiences and ideas. The woman was doing such challenging work, so similar to that for which Pat had devoted her life.

On the way back she told Eloy Anello, who was the native interpreter and organizer of that part of Camino del Sol, that she had never been on such a horrible road in all her years. To get her mind off the roads, she turned her attention to llamas that were being tended on the terraced mountainsides. Driving from the civilized city of Cochabamba to the small community of Pasto Grande and on to the tin-producing town of Oruro, the roads got better and better. They seemed downright beautiful by the time they reached the radio station outside Oruro, and during the three-hour drive to the city of La Paz.

The magical journey continued back to the Peruvian border and Lake Titicaca and on to Santa Cruz. The next stop was in Guayana before the group finally got back to the United States and Pat to her beloved Reservation home in South Dakota.

This was a monumental journey for Pat in many ways. Perhaps the most distinctive moment was the one in Misque Pampa when she accepted the Bahá'í Faith in her heart. She has said that her recognition of Bahá'u'lláh was not an intellectual process. What reached her was the love she received from complete strangers in the rarefied heights of the Andes. She saw this as an echo of God's universal Messenger and believed it could unite people from all the extremes of the earth. Yes, there were still questions, but it was there, high in the heavens, that her heart was touched.

XIV

Patricia and the Bahá'í Faith

The experience at Misque Pampa, Peru was Pat's moment of acceptance of the Bahá'í Faith, but she did not enroll in the Faith then. There were still barriers to overcome and veils to be removed.

Eloy Anello was her major teacher while she was in South America. At one of his meetings she met Badi Foster, a young Bahá'í who had grown up in Africa. They were sitting on an ottoman when, after some smalltalk, Badi asked her why she wasn't a Bahá'í. He said, "and your problem is?" She said she believed in reincarnation.

Badi asked if she believed Bahá'u'lláh was Who He said He was. She said she did. Bahá'ís regard Bahá'u'lláh as the most recent Messenger from God in a line of progressive revelations that include Abraham, Zoroaster, Moses, Buddha, Christ, Muhammad, and a few others. Then he offered, "You say that you believe in reincarnation, and Bahá'u'lláh does not support that. Therefore, you are not becoming a Bahá'í." She said, "Yes."

"Isn't that awfully arrogant of you?" he asked.

She was so taken aback by this simple and direct question that so clearly revealed her own inconsistency that she had to think for a minute before quietly answering: "Yes it is."[88]

It was fitting that Badi used a tool that she knew and had used often and well. She was not one to argue but loved to present a mirror in which people could clearly see the flaws in their thinking for themselves. Badi held that mirror before her and said no more. A major veil evaporated and she realized that Bahá'u'lláh was the authority. She still had questions but she never again challenged anything Bahá'u'lláh said. Later questions were probes for understanding. The ability to ask questions is considered one of the greatest gifts from God. In the Bahá'í view, questions open the way to knowledge, understanding, insights, and contribute to wisdom. A major Bahá'í principle is an unfettered search for truth. She continued to learn as much as she could from Eloy before returning north.

There was one more stop before returning home. That was in Guayana. There, she met a young Guyanese Indian artist and musician who had recently enrolled in the Faith. His name was Guy Marco, and he became their driver. That was the beginning of a bond that was so strong that Pat often referred to Guy as her son. Like Pat, Guy was concerned with the loss of language and culture among indigenous people. He referred to this as "the second killing of the Indians."[89] They shared the vision of not going back into the past culturally, but carrying the culture into the future with its unique contributions to the human family. They met many times in different parts of the world later on and she would invariably introduce him as her son.

Even though she had not enrolled as a Bahá'í, her commitment to the Faith was strong and she was eager to do what she could to contribute to its defense and progress. Some people on the Pine Ridge Reservation were persecuting the Bahá'ís and saying they should leave. People would complain of the Bahá'ís, saying, "All they were doing was trying to convert us—just another group trying to convert us." Pine Ridge had been Jacqueline's home and Pat, who was not a Bahá'í, offered to interview Jacqueline and write a rebuttal. She wrote a two-part article for the local newspaper. People called Jacqueline, saying they had read the articles and it helped them understand so much. Jacqueline said, "That was Pat's way of defending the Faith before she was a Bahá'í."

Pat complained to Kevin that she had not met enough Bahá'ís in the United States. The only ones she knew were Kevin and Jacqueline. She wanted to meet some ordinary Bahá'ís.

Pat actually knew quite a few Bahá'ís, but was not aware of it. In her travels with Kevin she would often be introduced to his friends who happened to be Bahá'ís. She just thought of them as Kevin's friends.

One such person was Dorothy Nelson, a federal judge on the 9th Circuit Court of Appeals. When they were first introduced it was stressed for Dorothy's benefit that Pat was "very, very interested in the law."[90] Dorothy took the bait and when she got home she sent Pat a book on Indian law written by a fellow judge on the 9th Circuit Court. Pat was pleased with the book and that was the start of a life-long correspondence and friendship.

Several people have described the relationship between Dorothy and Pat as "two peas in a pod." It has been said that hearing one talk was like an echo of the other. They had attended UCLA at the same time, although Dorothy was slightly ahead of Pat. Both had been swimmers on the aquatic ballet swim team, but at different times. Pat remembered writing to Dorothy about some issue when Dorothy was vicepresident of the student body. There was a brief exchange of letters, but they never met. Both had been energetic and committed political activists before becoming Bahá'ís, and upon becoming Bahá'ís, each changed her view of how to make a better world.

Pat started reading Kevin's Bahá'í books and asked a lot of questions of both Kevin and Jacqueline. She wanted to meet more Bahá'ís, so she asked Kevin when the next conference was going to be. There was a National Convention coming up and Kevin said she could meet a lot of Bahá'ís there. She decided to go.

Kevin and his mother had to drive more than 100 miles to the Bismarck, North Dakota airport to catch a plane to Chicago to attend the Convention. Somewhere along the way Kevin casually mentioned that she could not attend any of the sessions because they were for Bahá'ís only, but that she could meet a lot of Bahá'ís in the hotel lobby.

Pat then asked what she had to do to go in to the sessions. Kevin explained that she needed to be an enrolled Bahá'í. She asked how to do that. He said she had to sign an enrollment card. She told him to get one for her. He happened to have one and gave it to his mother, who immediately signed it.

Jacqueline Left Hand Bull said that on that same night she had a vivid dream of Pat saying, "Jacqueline, I want to tell you I am a Bahá'í." In the dream Pat repeated the statement three times so that Jacqueline would understand that it was true and she meant it. When Jacqueline woke up, the phone was ringing with the news. Jacqueline reported: ". . . and sure enough Pat had signed her card."[91]

Pat's first experience as an enrolled Bahá'í was to attend a National Convention. She got her wish of meeting many Bahá'ís, including Jim and Dorothy Nelson, whom she had met before without realizing that they, too, were members of the Faith.

After enrolling in the Bahá'í Faith, Pat got calls from all over the country, some praising and some condemning her. There was a call from Jacqueline's father, who told Pat he was very disappointed in her. That was the end of his admiration for her. He said she had abandoned the Indian ways.

Throughout the world Christians, Muslims, Jews, Buddhists, and American Indians and other aboriginal groups share the common fear that when someone from their group accepts the Bahá'í Faith they are abandoning their religion, culture, and traditions. Few realize that the coming of Bahá'u'lláh is, in fact, the fulfillment of all they cherished. When one becomes a Bahá'í, he or she is not giving up the former religion, but fulfilling it. The Bahá'í Faith is the fruition of what has been held dear, anticipated, and for which members of the culture were praying. Predictions and prophecies of all religions, traditions, and ancient ways from all over the world—in both recorded and oral history—find fulfillment in the Bahá'í Faith.

After enrolling in the Faith, Pat would spend time sitting on the riverbank with Kevin asking questions.[92] Dorothy Nelson also sent her more information on legal matters, especially concerning Supreme Court Justice Sandra Day O'Connor's views on Indian religions.*

In her early years as a Bahá'í, Pat absorbed all she could about the Faith and attended every conference or meeting possible. How-

---

* See Chapter XII

ever, her biggest shock came two-and-a-half years later in 1993. Tod Ewing had resigned from the National Spiritual Assembly when he was appointed a Continental Counselor. The National Spiritual Assembly is a nine-member body elected by Bahá'í delegates from throughout the forty-eight contiguous states and the District of Columbia. It is the highest administrative body for the Bahá'ís under this jurisdiction. Its purpose is to guide Bahá'í communities on a national level. Counselors are individuals appointed by the Universal House of Justice. They serve five-year terms in an advisory, but not administrative, capacity. People cannot serve both as a Counselor and on an administrative institution of the Faith at the same time. It was necessary for the delegates from the last election to elect a replacement.

Bahá'ís generally do not discuss or speculate on elections so there were no "front runners." All Bahá'í elections follow the same procedure. There are no parties or nominations. Campaigning and electioneering are strictly forbidden. Voters are called upon to pray, reflect, and vote only for those who best fulfill the standards set by the Guardian of the Faith, Shoghi Effendi, who said: "Hence it is incumbent upon the chosen delegates to consider without the least trace of passion and prejudice, and irrespective of any material consideration, the names of only those who can best combine the necessary qualities of unquestioned loyalty, of selfless devotion, of a well-trained mind, of recognized ability and mature experience."[93] Much to her surprise, if not consternation, Patricia was elected. In fact, it came as a surprise to most of the Bahá'ís of the United States because she was so new to the Faith. As Jack McCants, a well-traveled, well-known believer, and at the time a member of the National Spiritual Assembly, said, "I'd never even heard of her." [94]

Probably no one was more surprised than Patricia herself. She immediately turned to Dorothy for solace, who told her, "Patricia, you shouldn't be amazed because of your reputation for fairness and justice." But Patricia protested, "I'm such a young Bahá'í and I want to learn, help me, help me." Dorothy said they had a lot of e-mails and a lot of phone calls after that.

It was after her election to the National Spiritual Assembly that she indicated a clear preference for being called Patricia, although she never made a big issue of it. All her life she had been known as Pat. Still, she felt "Patricia" was more dignified, and in respect for the institution of the National Spiritual Assembly, it was more appropriate. However, even those who served with her on that body and knew of her preference called her "Pat." As Dorothy Nelson said, "Whenever I introduced her at any event, I always said 'Patricia.'" But Dorothy still speaks of her as "Pat." Because of this preference, she is referred to as Patricia for the rest of the book, except in direct quotes.

Being elected to the National Spiritual Assembly became an accelerated learning experience. Within a short period of time she went from being an advocate for Indian rights to being a champion for all human rights. But the biggest change came in the style of decision-making.

For decades Patricia had been effective in getting things done by using confrontation and manipulating power relationships. She knew the hard scrabble of the political world with its threats, cajoling, posturing, and deal-making. And she was good at it. All of a sudden, she was thrown into a high level decision-making system where decisions are made by consultation rather than confrontation. It is an entirely different process.

Confrontation is verbally slugging it out, by fair means or foul, to get your way. Whereas consultation calls for earnest, frank, and friendly discussion based on mutual trust and good will to arrive at the best possible decision. There are no entrenched positions and no winners and losers. All win when they work together to seek that which is best for all.

A primary consideration in Bahá'í consultation is promoting unity. That involves having respect for people with different views, and seeking and seriously listening to opinions different from your own, because they are different. Preconceived positions or a strong desire for a certain outcome are not appropriate.

Unity, in this context, calls for focusing on common objectives and purposes. Different opinions and points of view are essential to be shared and considered. This leads to better understanding so good decisions can be made. In confrontational decision-making, problems and ill feeling are often created over disagreements. Frequently, the spoken purpose is secondary. Even when there is a common objective, the means to achieve something are often carried out at the expense of what it is they are trying to achieve. It is common for partisan parties or groups to actively highlight or exaggerate points on which they disagree just to make the other party look bad. A compromise is sometimes agreed upon so the conflicting parties can have some resolution. The result is that frequently the best solution is never found. People accustomed to confrontation sometimes think of unity as a luxury of limited value once differences are settled. In the Bahá'í view, unity is an essential startingpoint needed to find the best solutions and to resolve differences. Rúhíyyih Khánum, the wife of Shoghi Effendi, who later became a friend of Patricia's, said she once had a concept about the unity of mankind that proved to be quite incorrect; she had thought that in the process of establishing this unity, you lost what you were, but she learned from Shoghi Effendi that "the concept of 'unity in diversity' is quite different; you keep what you are and bring the finest fruits of your own people, race, tribe, or whatever unit it may be, and contribute this to the pool for the benefit of all."[95]

Consultation is an important aspect of establishing and maintaining this unity. In consultation there are no liberals or conservatives, no progressives or traditionalists. Partisanship and entrenched positions have no place. Preconceived desires for a certain outcome interfere with finding the best answers. When there is proper consultation, the final decision is often a surprise—something no one had thought of before. It grows out of the discussion. Differing opinions are important, and they are to be openly expressed during the discussion. Once a decision is made, however, everyone is to support it no matter how he or she may have voted. This is more than passive or grudging approval. It means wholehearted support and doing what is necessary for the idea to work. Otherwise, if something does not work out, it will never be known if the idea was flawed or if lack of support made it fail.

It means seeing the difference between the ideas and the people who express them; being able to disagree without being disagreeable. Points of view are offered, not to persuade or convince, but as a contribution for a more complete understanding, in search of the best decision. This means stating opinions clearly and strongly, but with a detached motivation.

Once expressed, the idea belongs to the group and not just to the one who first voiced it. It is open for others to consider, and modifications almost always occur. Opinions tend to shift in the light of new information, understanding, insight, or perspectives. Discussion is both frank and courteous, without anyone giving or taking offense. It calls for the ability to change opinions easily as appropriate. In the end no one gets credit for the idea. It is a product of the group. As such everyone is to support the decision and try to make it work, no matter how he or she may have voted. If it does not work, appropriate changes can be made if all are united. Patricia caught on to the new system quickly and it soon became her preferred way of approaching issues.

James Nelson (Jim) was chairman of the National Spiritual Assembly at the time and Dorothy said that Patricia was very fond of him. Whenever she came upon something that she didn't understand, she would call Jim, and she took his word as gospel.

Finally Dorothy felt it was time to put that into perspective. She told Patricia, "Look, you've got to understand that we have no priest, no clergy, and even though he's the chair of the Assembly, his is an opinion."

Patricia said, "But he's always right." Dorothy said, "Well, I agree with you, but at any rate, you have to be careful that you take his word as the best of his knowledge."

Jim explained Patricia's transition this way, "The thing that I remember most about Pat is the way she went with the facts. She would change her mind in an instant, where others would hang on forever. She was the most flexible person I ever saw."[96]

Before becoming a Bahá'í, she had a political approach to the world; she was used to the interplay of pressures and counterpressures based on political climate or societal norms. That disappeared. She became truly convinced that consultation and the application of Bahá'í principles were the answer to world problems. The change came, as Jim Nelson went on to say, "More rapidly than anyone could imagine."

Dorothy Nelson reported that before Patricia was a Bahá'í, she was involved with Indian politics and fought for Indian rights and sovereignty by lobbying in Washington. It was all confrontational. After she learned about the consultative method, instead of going in to win at all costs with a clear winner and a loser at the end, she would go in and say, "Let's talk about this and let me give you my perspective, let me hear your perspective so that a just decision can be made." Before, as a lobbyist, she was pushing to get her point across with the attitude: "I'm here for Indian rights and I'm here to win."

Jack McCants explained: "There isn't any comparison to her for her development, her maturity, her understanding, her capacity to say things in a way to get your attention and leave a lasting impression about it. Her heart was in teaching Native American people. She knew the hurts and the needs of the community she came from. She wanted a listening ear and wanted to work towards solving the long-term problems."

She would mention her children and grandchildren during discussion in order to illustrate certain points. That brought the discussions down to the basic elements of life. Some people like to dwell on abstract principles to the point that you wonder what they are talking about. You couldn't do that around her. She would bring the subject right down to the real world—in a loving, kind, but wise way. She brought her experience as part of an oppressed minority with her, and always thought about how things would affect those closest to her. She would ask the question: "How will this benefit my people?" While never harsh, crude, demanding, or blaming, she opened the window to other ways of viewing the world.

When others would have difficulty understanding what she was saying, she would let it go. Then, much later, she would mention it again casually, and, when necessary, repeat it until people could understand her point without being pushy. The purpose was always for understanding, not persuasion. She really didn't talk much. She let others chatter on and on, but when she spoke, people listened because whatever she said was guaranteed to carry gems of wisdom.

She retained her skill of getting attention when needed. Several colleagues on the National Spiritual Assembly mentioned a time when they had just finished discussing something and were about to move on to the next subject. Patricia had something she wanted to say, but the others were not paying attention. They were busy shuffling papers in preparation for the next item on the agenda. She very quietly said, "I just love Charlie Barkley"—a highly controversial professional basketball player of the time. Singing the praises of this controversial athlete was so far removed from anything they had been talking about that, while others had only been half listening before, they were stunned by this comment, dropped what they were doing, stared at her, and paid rapt attention. Then, and only then, she smoothly went on to share what she had to say.

Persistent though she was, there was a kindness and gentleness in all she said or did. Jack considered her the personification of Bahá'u'lláh's admonition that words should always be cloaked with love and kindness so people would not take offense. Jack said, "Always, her words were clothed with—not just a word like *love*—but with respect and with earnest, honest feeling of concern and integrity behind it. You could feel it in her voice."

He went on to say that when she became a member of the National Spiritual Assembly ". . . it sure made a very positive difference; a very happy difference. I will put it that way. You can't talk about Pat without positive feelings surrounding your thoughts. You just can't do it. I can't imagine anybody having a negative response to her."

There is a tendency to think of members of groups you do not know much about as being similar. Through her, others came to realize there was not an "Indian" point of view or way of believing, behaving, or looking at things any more than there were German, French, American, or English, points of view. Her way of making that point was gentle and self-deprecating. She told of a time when she was speaking to an Indian tribe whose culture she did not understand. When they disagreed with what the speaker was saying, they would cross their fingers without saying anything. She saw members of the tribe crossing their fingers and she knew she had lost them. She quit talking, knowing that more words would make the matter worse. Only after learning more of their culture and understanding how they viewed the issue could she take up the discussion again. By use of this story, she got her point across without making anyone feel bad or guilty.

Everything she did was with energy and conviction. Others would follow her lead because of her enthusiasm and commitment, which was decisive but without fanfare. Anyone consulting with her had to appreciate and love her because she was always kind but firm and gentle. Yet she always got her point across without being controversial. She was wise in how she said things.

She often used humorous stories to make serious points. She had little patience with egotistical or boastful people. To illustrate the folly of self-importance, she loved the story of a land turtle that couldn't swim and was caught on a small island with rapidly rising water. Two eagles flying overhead saw its plight and told the turtle it was about to drown. The turtle said, "You could save me." When asked how, the turtle told them to get a large stick and each one grab one end. They were to bring it to the turtle, who would clamp his jaws on the middle of the stick and the two eagles could fly away with the turtle hanging on.

The two eagles did this and it worked well. They were flying away with the turtle clinging to the stick when another eagle flew by and said, "What a brilliant idea. Whose idea was that?"

The self-important turtle could not resist. He opened his mouth to say, "Miiiiinnne" and let go of the stick, plunging into the swirling waters below.

In 1994 the National Spiritual Assembly of the United States was asked to go to Haifa, Israel to confer with the Universal House of Justice. The Universal House of Justice is the highest administrative body of the Bahá'í world. With headquarters in Haifa, Israel, this nine-member body is elected by the members of the more than 180 National Spiritual Assemblies from all over the world.

The members of the National Spiritual Assembly were invited to the house of 'Abdu'l-Bahá to have dinner with Rúhíyyih Khánum. 'Abdu'l-Bahá was the eldest son of Bahá'u'lláh, Who appointed Him as the Center of the Bahá'í Covenant and interpreter of His Word. With the passing of 'Abdu'l-Bahá in 1921, Shoghi Effendi, his eldest grandson, was appointed Guardian of the Faith and continued to live in the house of 'Abdu'l-Bahá. Today the house is visited by Bahá'ís from around the world during their pilgrimages and is maintained much like it was in the days of 'Abdu'l-Bahá.

Rúhíyyih Khánum was one of a few exceptional Bahá'ís who were given the designation of Hand of the Cause—the highest station that could be bestowed upon a Bahá'í. She was also the widow of the Guardian, Shoghi Effendi. It is safe to say she was one of the most prominent, highly respected, and best-known Bahá'ís in the world at that time.

After dinner they went into the drawing room and Khánum said, "I want Patricia Locke to sit next to me as a sign of high respect." Patricia was stunned. She was the junior member of the National Spiritual Assembly, having been a member for less than a year, and did not feel worthy of such an honor. It reflected Khánum's feeling of the importance of indigenous people and the need to pay special attention to them for the purpose of encouraging them so their voices and contributions could be shared.

Khánum developed this attitude from the influence of the Guardian. She once said, "He was the only one who got excited and could see the importance of the first this or that (members of different ethnic groups) to embrace the faith."[97] That attitude played a definite, important, and lifelong role in Khánum's becoming a champion of oppressed people from all corners of the world. Her worldwide travels included audiences with kings, emperors, presidents, and other dignitaries of many countries, as well visits to remote villages in Africa, Asia, the Americas, and various islands of the Pacific that had neither plumbing nor electricity. As a result, Khánum was dearly loved throughout the world and had been adopted by countless aboriginal peoples in many parts of sub-Sahara Africa, on numerous islands of the Pacific, and by Native tribes in the Americas from Alaska to Chile. Honoring Patricia this way, by offering her the closest seat, spoke volumes of her deep concern for the underheard and underrepresented members of the human family.

In 1995 Patricia traveled with Juana Conrad and the Nelsons as members of the National Spiritual Assembly to the United Nations Conference on Women held in Beijing, China. The group visited a dance class in one of the Chinese cities and Patricia demonstrated a technique from the ballet lessons of her youth, a stretching exercise using a wooden pole horizontally affixed to a mirrored wall. The youngsters were delighted by this demonstration.

While in China, they also did some sightseeing before the conference and Patricia bought a beautiful cloisonné cane. When the day came for the session on indigenous people, Patricia appeared, walking in her natural, regal manner, dressed in her Lakota finery with beautiful cowboy boots and brandishing her new, elegant cane. She looked like royalty. Considering her majestic entrance and her worldwide reputation of working for indigenous rights, her election as chair of the conference was a surprise to no one.

Several propositions were made that were strident, accusative, and demanding. As chair, Patricia had the task of refining them before they were voted on. Again, she turned to the Nelsons for help asking, "How could we phrase this in Bahá'í language?" They would work on things together, but both Nelsons affirmed that most of the revisions were hers. Much of what came out of that caucus into formal resolutions, particularly about the rights of women and girls, were changed from being negative and demanding to having a positive tone. This was a deliberate change from the accusatory way in which the ideas were first presented to one that showed forward thinking that was positive and uplifting.

Patricia's work was well-known among those working for human rights. The Dali Lama invited her, along with Jacqueline Left Hand Bull and a few other people, for a two-hour meeting. He obviously

knew quite a bit about Patricia's work and praised what she was doing. Before the session was over, he presented her with a white scarf
and kissed her on the cheek.[98]

Patricia's beloved Rúhíyyih Khánum died on January 19, 2000.
Patricia was devastated. She and Jack McCants attended the funeral
as official representatives of the National Spiritual Assembly of the
United States. Jack said, "Her death was very hard for Pat. She really
felt that the only person who really spoke up for the Indians had
died. She just felt sort of abandoned." She would lament, "Now who
will stick up for the indigenous people of the world?"

An example of the quality of the contributions Patricia made was
shown at a Bahá'í conference in Milwaukee in the summer of 2001.
In the opening session, Bill Davis, who was then chair of the National Spiritual Assembly, announced to the more than 13,000 Bahá'ís
gathered that originally a smaller conference, just for youth, had been
planned. He reported that Patricia raised the question: "Why would
you want a conference for youth and not invite their families?" After
a few moments of silence to reflect on the profound magnitude and
implications of that simple question, the event was changed to a
family conference.

This proved to be her final contribution. She became ill on the last
day of that gathering and never fully recovered.

In all matters, it was her simple, honest, and profound insight that
had such a monumental impact on all who were fortunate enough
to be near her.

XV

Her Passing[99]

The last year and a half of Patricia's life were especially difficult. It started when her beloved grandson, Hepana, was killed in an automobile accident when he was on his way to Wakpala to visit his grandmother. According to Kevin, "In my way of thinking the thing that really took her down was when Hepana died in the car wreck. She really had a rapid decline after that."

Then there was the passing of Rúhíyyih Khánum, which was devastating for Patricia. Khánum had been a model for her, and the woman she considered the major champion of the aborigines of the world, and she was gone. Patricia's own powers were waning and she was deeply concerned about who would now speak for those with no voice. Something precious went out of her life.

Another serious problem had to do with her legs. When she was younger, she had a problem with her legs that most people would not consider a problem. She was a beautiful woman and when dressed for swimming or tennis, men she didn't know would stare and ogle her legs because they were gorgeous. As she told Winona, "Oh, my legs cause me great problems." One reason she wore cowboy boots was to cover her legs to avoid the crude remarks and stares of strange men.

Now there was a different kind of a problem with her legs: diabetes. During the last decade of her life she had gained a lot of weight, and diabetes flared up. Her mother had died when she was in her fifties and, although undiagnosed, it was thought that she had died of complications from diabetes. Patricia now had to deal with an agonizing decision: should her legs be amputated? The circulation was such that she could hardly walk. Most of her final summer was spent in bed.

Even though she was feeling less energetic, she was still fully engaged with life and spent much time on the phone. There was a powwow coming up and her cousin Robert End of Horn, Sr., was eager that she go. She hesitated because it was so hard for her to get around. Kevin offered to take her in a wheelchair, so she went. At one point Robert tricked her into coming onto the dance circle. When she got to the circle, with Kevin pushing her wheelchair, Robert announced a song dedicated to her. Kevin wheel-danced her around the circle to an honor she never would have consented to if she had known what Robert had planned. It was marvelous! People swarmed onto the dance circle to shake her hand while she was dancing in her wheelchair. It proved to be her final powwow.

As mentioned in the previous chapter, a family conference was scheduled by the National Spiritual Assembly to be held in Milwaukee, Wisconsin, from June 28 through July 1, 2001. Of course, she went. It proved to be both the final example of the kind of contributions she made in consultation and her last major Bahá'í event.

After the conference she returned to Wakpala, and one day her friend Gary Kimble called. He invited her to the San Carlos Apache Reservation near Globe, Arizona, for a special retreat he was giving for Indian spiritual leaders. Again she was hesitant to go because she was having so much trouble getting around, but Gary was insistent. Kevin offered to take her, so they went.

They flew to Phoenix, rented a car, and drove to Globe. She used a walker and had a wonderful time. Here were some of her dearest Indian friends with whom she had worked so hard for so many years on a wide variety of important issues: Indian education, Indian self-determination and rights, language, and artifact and sacred site preservation. During the retreat, they laughed and consulted on a lot of different topics and had many prayers. She was delighted to be with her friends at this meeting in such an elevated spiritual atmosphere, and with such a high spiritual level of consultation.

One night they had a special Apache dish that contained hot peppers. Soon after dinner she had an upset stomach and Kevin took her to the San Carlos Hospital. The doctor examined her vital signs and saw something more serious than an upset stomach. Medevac was called from Phoenix. A helicopter quickly arrived and she was taken to the Indian hospital in Phoenix. From there, she was transferred to the Maricopa County Hospital where she spent the last seven weeks of her life.

Kevin drove their rental car back to Phoenix, and Winona came to Phoenix from Wakpala. The two of them stayed at the home of a friend, Steve Gonzalas, and spent as much time as they could with their mother in the hospital.

It was increasingly clear that her legs would have to be amputated: a prospect that weighed heavily on her heart and mind. Nonetheless, it was inevitable. Circulation had stopped and the leg tissues were dying.

She was conscious most of the time she was in the hospital, but she was hooked up to so many tubes that she could not speak. She would point and use sign language to communicate. People had difficulty knowing what she wanted. Someone suggested that she should draw pictures and she was given a piece of paper and a pencil. To make people happy, but with her sense of humor intact, she drew a picture of an arrow and pointed with that.

Also, with her good humor, she would point outside to let people know that what she really wanted was a cigarette. Alas, that was not to be in the smoke-free hospital.

Surgery was performed and both legs were amputated above the knees. She was stoically recovering, was moved from the ICU into a minimal care facility, and rehab was started. Even with her missing legs she was upbeat and friendly, and retained much of her old spirit.

She was in the hospital on the 11th of September when the Twin Towers were attacked in New York. She noticed that people were wearing a lot of red, white, and blue and were being extra patriotic and she wanted to know what was going on. Kevin wanted to avoid anything that would place more stress on his mother so he answered her questions in such a way as to shield her from news of the atrocity, which he felt would have only added to her burden. Rehabilitation was continuing well and there was even talk about returning home.

Kevin made a trip to Wakpala. His mother gave him a strange request. He knew that he had an older sister who died shortly after her birth. Though he was aware that the remains had been cremated and that his mother had kept them with her all those years, he didn't know where they were located. His mother told him exactly where the remains were and told him to bring the ashes to Phoenix with him when he returned.

On October 19, 2001, Winona and Kevin were making a normal visit to the hospital and left about 9 p.m. About four o'clock the next morning, they received a phone call that they should return to the hospital because Patricia was not doing well. There was fear that she would not survive much longer, so Kevin immediately set off for the hospital.

When he got there she had been hooked up to the respirator and other equipment was needed to keep her lungs and heart going because there was no longer any sign of brain activity. Kevin waited until Winona could get to the hospital and then the two of them made the decision to remove life-support.

The immediate cause of death was listed as a heart attack with the vascular leg problem being a contributing factor. That was the morning of October 20, which, for Bahá'ís in the Western world, is a special date, because that is the day they celebrate the birth of the Báb, Who was a forerunner of Bahá'u'lláh. Bahá'ís believe the Báb and Bahá'u'lláh to be Twin Manifestations for this age. It was as if she chose a date for death that would focus attention away from her.

The local Spiritual Assembly of Phoenix directed Kevin to a reliable funeral home that would permit Bahá'ís to make the preparations for the body. It is normal in the western world for undertakers to complete the final arrangements, including preparation of the body.

They are the professionals and generally do a good job providing much needed comfort during highly stressful times in peoples' lives.

However, Bahá'ís have special provisions for taking care of the dead. Many Bahá'ís prefer to perform the task themselves. Most regard this as a spiritual bounty and responsibility. According to Bahá'í law, preparation of the body includes prayerfully washing and wrapping the body in a shroud and placing a special ring on the dead person's finger. Often, many prayers are shared and soft music is played during this time. There is to be no embalming and burial is to take place within an hour's journey from the place of death.

Kevin and Patricia's dear friend from Alaska, Art Davidson, performed this service of preparing the body for burial. While washing the body, Kevin reflected on the Bahá'í burial practice. It occurred to him that many people have the undertakers do this, since they are the ones who know what do to. But Kevin and Art felt they were experiencing something special. Kevin said that what kept going through his mind was, "It was such a sacred trust; a sacred responsibility to handle that." He added, "The body is the vehicle for the human spirit for the short period of time that we have on earth. So . . . the thing that kept going through my mind was this sacred trust. I didn't know what to do. You just get started and you have to do something, so you just take off and take care of it." They agreed that she had fought the good fight and accomplished in one lifetime what most people could not do given many lifetimes. She was proactive and did many outstanding things in her life.

Niela Redford was a nurse during those final days, and she had a special interest in Patricia. Even though she had not known Patricia before she was in the hospital, she performed two outstanding services. First of all, she saw to it that Patricia's legs were frozen so that when it came time for her burial, her legs could be buried with her. The legs, together with the ashes of her first child, were placed in the coffin. Kevin and Art then placed a star quilt over the body.*

---

* See Chapter XIV for an explanation of the significance of the star quilt.

The other special thing Niela did took place later. Patricia had told her that her uncle Joe had been sent to Phoenix because of tuberculosis and died there. Patricia wanted to know where her uncle was buried. A few years later Niela informed the family of Joe's burial place, and that he was buried close to his niece. She described the location and even sent a photograph of the grave.

Patricia's funeral lasted over three hours, with people coming from all over the country to pay their final respects.*

During the following year, many things were done on the Reservation in the name of Patricia to honor her memory and help her along her journey in the next world.

There is probably no more fitting eulogy and summary of Patricia's life than her own last written words. Rhonda Palmer had been Rúhíyyih Khánum's nurse during her last days and even though she did not know Patricia, she had offered to stay with her during her final hours because of a dream she had of Rúhíyyih Khánum. Rhonda felt Khánum was telling her to take care of Patricia during her final illness.

Patricia's Gravestone

* See Chapter I.

Following is an account she gave of Patricia's last writing:

The next night she was pensive. It was difficult for her to write, but she asked for some paper and a pen. For more than an hour she labored over her writing, and finally lay back in the bed, exhausted, but having finished her work. On the paper in small handwriting were these words:

To the Bahá'í Youth of the world: We come to you in loving consultation.

Signed, the Locke family.

XVI

Distinctions

With all that Patricia did, anyone who knew her and is reading this might be struck by what has not been said. Volumes could be written about her achievements, even though she made little note of them. Her life was focused on things to be accomplished, not on honors won. People might disagree as to what should be mentioned in a biography, but anyone who knew her would agree that the list of distinctions is long and impressive. The following items, listed in chronological order, are clearly among the most notable items of recognition.

1. Circa 1970, receiving her Lakota name: Tȟawáčhiŋ Wašté Wíŋ.
2. 1991, receiving the MacArthur Fellowship award.
3. 1993, election to the National Spiritual Assembly of the Baháʼís of the United States; 2001 elected vice-chair.
4. 2005, posthumous induction into the National Women's Hall of Fame.

These four have several things in common. First of all, no one can seek any of them. They are not things for which anyone can apply, nor are they things for which anyone can aspire. In each case some individual or group feels strongly that the person is worthy of fulfilling the role.

She wore each honor lightly. No one knows what was most important to her, but the one she would mention most was her Lakota name, and even then she would speak of it for instruction and not self-aggrandizement. The honors never changed her. She remained the same Patricia—cooking for grandchildren, helping her neighbors, and always feeding the dogs.

It is true that she tried hard to live up to her Lakota name, and that the money from the MacArthur award enabled her to do things she could not have done otherwise. To her host of friends, relatives, and acquaintances, she remained the cherished woman she had always been. She remained a regular patron at the Mobridge library; continued serving on the board of the Reservation radio station, KLND; still had her many dogs on which she doted; and often took in strangers who needed a place to stay. Through it all, her children and grandchildren remained her highest priority.

Tȟawáčhiŋ Wašté Wíŋ (Compassionate Woman)

In addition to what was said in Chapter XI, it is worth noting that many more mementos of this event were among her belongings than any other recognition she received. In part that may be because it fit in so well with her strong conviction on the importance of the preservation of cultural heritage.

The MacArthur Fellows Program or MacArthur Fellowship

This is sometimes called "The Genius Award," "The MacArthur Genius Award," or simply "The MacArthur." It is an award given by the John D. and Catherine T. MacArthur Foundation each year to twenty to forty U.S. residents who "show exceptional merit and promise for continued and enhanced creative work." The recipients are singled out for the award, and a monetary reward is provided for them to be able to continue their work without the need to worry about financial pressures. In every field, the MacArthur is known as the pinnacle of success.

According to the Foundation website, "the fellowship is not a reward for past accomplishment, but rather an investment in a person's originality, insight, and potential." It does not matter in what field they are working, or in what capacity. As of 2007, there had been 756 recipients who had received a total of more than $350 million.

Patricia received $300,000, paid out quarterly over a number of years. All that is said about her in the list of recipients is "Tribal Leader." However, the director of the program has said, "Pat Locke personified the spirit of our program by carrying out her work in education with creativity, dignity and skill."[100]

No one can apply for the award. People are nominated anonymously by a body of nominators who are on the lookout for potential candidates. A small selection committee of about a dozen people whose names are not made public review the recommendations. The committee makes its recommendations to the President and the Board of Directors of the foundation, which makes the final selection. The entire process is anonymous and confidential. It has been discovered that a Chippewa leader from White Earth, Minnesota, suggested her name to one of the nominators because of the impact she had made on his Reservation. He knew that she had done the same for others. A friend of Patricia's was talking with one of the members of the committee after Patricia got the award and asked the committee member about it. All she would say is that in Patricia's case it was clear to everyone who reviewed the material that she perfectly fit the criteria and deserved the award.

Most new MacArthur Fellows first learn they have even been considered when they receive the congratulatory phone call. This was true of Patricia. The call was news to her. It is unlikely that she had ever given a moment's thought to it before then. Most people who knew her well and were aware of the MacArthur were not surprised when she received it.

However, two problems were created by the award. One was jealousy and the other was requests for money. Several Indian men were outraged that she got it. They maintained that if an Indian was to get the award, it should have been one of them. One woman of considerable capacity and accomplishment with whom Patricia had worked tirelessly and closely in years past became quite nasty, not only toward Patricia, but toward her family. She would loudly proclaim to anyone who would listen, "I can't see why she was selected." Patricia did not react to these attacks, except when her grandchildren were the target. Then all she would say in response to negative comments was simply: "Oh, that was just alcohol speaking."[101]

The second problem had to do with requests for money. The MacArthur Foundation has no conditions as to how the money is to be spent. That is up to the individual who receives it. They answer to no one. However, the intent is clear: "to enable the recipient to more easily carry on creative work."

Patricia was living on the poverty-stricken Reservation, where unemployment is chronically high—often over 50%. The vast majority of people have a living standard that is unimaginable to much of middle-America. It would be natural for people who were so poor to think that she had become fabulously rich. Many of them had wonderful ideas of what could and should be done with Patricia's newfound wealth. Her response to people who wanted to use her money for their purposes—no matter how worthy—was straightforward, simple, and honest. She would say: "That is not what the money was intended for."

She found many creative ways to use the money. Typically, she worked on several projects at the same time. With the award money she could do even more. The money helped her expand her work in the areas of language, cultural, and sacred site preservation. She also dabbled in environmental issues. Mainly, she broadened her activities from Indian self-determination to wide-ranging and world-encompassing women's issues and other matters of universal human rights, especially concerning indigenous people.

Member and Vice-Chair of the National Spiritual Assembly of the Bahá'ís of the United States

When Patricia was elected vice-chair, she was the first American Indian elected as one of the body's senior officers in its nearly eighty years of existence.* It should be noted that the position is not honorary, but has specific duties. There was some description of Bahá'í elections in Chapter XIV, but it is worth repeating that elections take place without nominations, electioneering, or campaigning. Instead the process calls for prayer and reflection on the part of those voting.

Much of the significance of her election lies in the fact that all of her life she had been fighting to enable Indians to take their rightful place in human affairs. While Bahá'ís work diligently to remove all traces of prejudice from their activities, this distinction reflects that for which she had devoted her life. She was elected neither because of, nor in spite of, being an Indian, but because those voting for her, without the least trace of coercion or pressure, thought she was the right person for the responsibilities involved.

The National Women's Hall of Fame

Unlike the other distinctions, this one is strictly honorary. This prestigious organization was created in 1969 by a group of people in Seneca Falls, New York in commemoration of, and at the location of, the first Women's Rights Convention in 1848. The mission of the National Women's Hall of Fame is "to honor in perpetuity those women, citizens of the United States of America, whose contributions to the arts, athletics, business, education, government, the humanities, philanthropy and science, have been the greatest value for the development of their country."

The National Women's Hall of Fame inducts distinguished American women through a rigorous national honors selection process in-

---

* Since then Jacqueline Left Hand Bull, also a Lakota Indian, has been elected chairperson of the National Spiritual Assembly of the Bahá'ís of the United States.

volving representatives of many of the nation's important organizations and areas of expertise. Women are chosen for inclusion on the basis of the change they created that affects the social, economic, or cultural aspects of society; the significant national or global impact and result of change due to their achievement; and the enduring value of their achievement or change.

The woman who submitted Patricia's name confided in Kevin that, in her judgment, Patricia had accomplished so much and did so many things that affected and improved the lives of so many people that it was unthinkable that she was not listed in the National Women's Hall of Fame. The woman felt compelled to submit an application in Patricia's behalf. And, of course, the board of directors agreed and she was so honored.

In addition to what has been on the preceding pages, the biographical sketch associated with her induction to the Women's Hall of Fame listed many other achievements:

Instructor, curricula designer, and executive of the International Native Languages Institute

Chair of the American Indian Advisory Committee of the Martin Luther King, Jr. Holiday Commission

Wrote or contributed to more than two dozen published articles, not counting the series for the *Mobridge Tribune*

Served as a member of many advisory boards of organizations dedicated to social justice, human rights, and environmental issues

Developed policies, procedures, and education codes for Indian regions of the country

Co-chaired the United States Department of Interior Task Force on Indian Education Policy

Helped develop a Bureau of Indian Affairs Mission Statement and policies that were written into statute

Strong voice for tribal independence in deciding how and what Native American children should study.[102]

Her extensive international activities and achievements were not even mentioned.

Reaction

According to Kevin, Patricia was never impressed by people with lofty titles or those who paraded long lists of accomplishments. To her these were trappings and not the essence of the individual or what she or he was trying to accomplish. Working with legislative or government bureaucracies, she saw a big difference between those who had titles and those who got things done. She had little time for the titled incompetents and would concentrate on the doers. She also had little patience for people who may have earned a doctorate in some field and insisted on being called "doctor." She reasoned that was their training and preparation. But she would ask herself, what can they do?

This attitude carried over to accolades she received. For instance, when asked why she had received the MacArthur, her typical response was, "It was because I fed the dogs." That simple response spoke volumes about Patricia. That self-effacing remark not only reflected her modesty but, in a subtle way, the importance of living up to her Lakota name. She never paraded her list of achievements or used prestigious recognition to impress people or try to gain some advantage. She knew many prominent people well, but never indulged in namedropping. She didn't dwell on past achievements, except as learning experiences. Her gaze was on what needed to be done and doing it.

Her humility was well-illustrated by her friend of many years, Gary Kimble. He said, "I was one of Pat Locke's closest friends and there was much I never knew until after she died." He went on to talk about the work she did for the tribal college legislation, but then he said, "Little did I know that was only part of the reason she got the MacArthur Fellow. Because she was very, very discreet about this . . . I knew that she was a Bahá'í, but didn't know that she was on the governing board of Bahá'ís. And that's a very important thing to remember because that really covers everything." Even though he was not a Bahá'í, he spoke about the great spiritual significance of her election. He went on to say, ". . . much of the work that she was doing was very profound and she sought no publicity."[103]

Even her grandchildren, who were such an important part of her life and traveled with her to various parts of the world, were unaware of the vast scope of her work. For them her funeral was a revelation into the effectiveness of this woman whom they loved so dearly, but whose life had so many facets and dimensions completely unknown to them.

She never thought of recognition as a goal or even a milestone. Righting wrongs; improving lives; emancipating the oppressed— these were the challenges that fueled her activity, not a desire for recognition.

It wasn't that she was reluctant to talk about her accomplishments when appropriate. She would, matter-of-factly, without a hint of ego, mention these things as needed. She was so confident and comfortable with herself that she felt no need to broadcast her achievements.

Perhaps the greatest distinction of all was her life. Her satisfaction came from helping, not only her people, but all those who have been oppressed or downtrodden, to fulfill their own dreams and potential. Her goal was that all members of the human family should be able to freely give of their talents and capacities for the betterment of all mankind.

XVII

Tributes and Remembrances

Both during her funeral and afterward, a flood of spontaneous and heartfelt tributes poured forth. These came from institutions and a wide range of individuals from all walks of life. Following are some of those tributes and remembrances.

From the Universal House of Justice
(Addressed to the National Spiritual Assembly
of the United States):
We were deeply saddened by the news of the passing of highly devoted, self-sacrificing servant of the Cause, Patricia Locke. Her many years of dedicated service to the Faith as a member of your (U.S.) National Spiritual Assembly will long be remembered. The widespread recognition of her outstanding endeavors as an educator and administrator in championing the special educational needs of American Indians has contributed to the rising prestige of the Cause in the United States.

Kindly convey our loving sympathy to her family, and assure them of our heartfelt prayers at the Sacred Threshold for the progress of her illumined soul throughout the heavenly realms.

From the National Spiritual Assembly of the Bahá'ís of the United States:

The National Spiritual Assembly was stricken with grief and a sense of profound loss in the passing of our noble hearted dearly loved sister, Patricia Locke.

Patricia's life was a testament to the power of faith and transcendence, rising above all obstacles to found colleges for Indian peoples, to develop national educational policy and to promote human rights and environmental issues on every continent of the world, and to develop tribal education codes, language policy, and education departments for American Indian Nations throughout North America. A recipient of the distinguished MacArthur Fellowship, she was recognized throughout the world for her vision of human service and social development leading to her citation as one of the most influential Indian people of the 20th century.

After declaring her belief in the Faith of Bahá'u'lláh, Patricia traveled the globe sharing the Bahá'í principles of unity and equality and championing the upliftment of every soul and nation. She was elected to the National Spiritual Assembly of the Bahá'ís of the United States and was the first American Indian to be elected to that body to serve as an officer when she was elected Vice-Chair. Patricia will be long remembered for her sterling character, for her wit and charm, for her extraordinary compassion and kindness, and for her commitment to lifelong learning. She is a model for all women. Her most precious quality was her wholehearted devotion to her children, grandchildren and great-grandchildren about whom she made constant reference with expressions of love and celebrations of their lives.

Our lives have been enriched immeasurably by our love and association with dear Patricia. We offer prayers for the comfort and solace of the family and friends grieving the loss of such a precious soul.

From the National Spiritual Assembly of the Bahá'ís of Canada:

Dear Pat's indomitable spirit, her strength of character, and her unwavering, wholehearted commitment to the highest principles and noble ideals, will be sorely missed. Through decades of devoted service, she gave expression to all these qualities in distinguished service. The signal contributions she made both to the development of the Bahá'í community and for the betterment of indigenous peoples will be noted with special gratitude by future generations. That her qualities of spirit are so amply reflected through her children stands paramount in the considerable legacy she leaves us.

Though we mourn the loss of her physical presence, our sorrow is tempered in the knowledge that she has now been freed from the limitations of this earthly existence to raise her banner in the divine realm, her spirit undoubtedly rejoicing after her long and faithful labours in this world.

We take special comfort in Bahá'u'lláh's loving assurance that ". . . the soul, after its separation from the body, will continue to progress until it attaineth the presence of God, in a state and condition which neither the revolution of ages and centuries, nor the changes and chances of this world, can alter. It will endure as long as the Kingdom of God, His sovereignty, His dominion and power will endure. It will manifest the signs of God and His attributes, and will reveal His loving kindness and bounty." (*Gleanings from the Writings of Bahá'u'lláh*, p. 155)

Cindy Catches

(Patricia first met Cindy in Florida. Later, Cindy married a man from South Dakota, and the two women stayed in close contact with each other):

The most noble person that I have even been blessed to know in my life is Patricia Locke. Just thinking about her, I want to sit up straighter and be a better human being. That is what she inspired in those that were fortunate enough to be able to call her a friend and / or a mentor. She was both to me, and my life is more because I knew her.

I first met Pat when she would travel with her son Kevin's family going to the Miccosukee powwow every winter. I had heard that Kevin was a Bahá'í and I would try to organize a spiritual evening where we would feast on food and spiritual stories during the pow-wow. We formed a dear relationship. Sometimes I would be blessed as their family would stop at my home for a few days on their way home. Again we would have a gathering at my home to invite people to hear about the Bahá'í Faith from Kevin and we would always have Pat share with us as well. She wasn't a Bahá'í at that time. But she was a born educator and a bridge for the white people to have a better understanding of her beloved indigenous peoples of the world. She would kindly help us to understand, by sharing her own mistakes that she made, . . . how different cultures were, and how what is considered right by one, is not considered right by another.

I remember her sharing a story with me about her trip up to Canada where she was attending an elders' gathering. There was this young arrogant white man there who was being so disrespectful to the elders that she just couldn't stand it anymore. So she went up to this young man and just let him have it! This elder was watching her and when the young man left he called her over. "Young woman, you have been in that white world too long. You have forgotten yourself. These people are our guest on this Turtle Island (North America). They are still very young. You must show much more patience and compassion with them." And yes, I believe this to be the truth.

I remember her calling me, very concerned because the National Congress of American Indians had ask(ed) her to come and help pass a law to protect the religious freedom of Native Americans. Religious freedom had been against the law for Native Americans until 1979, and the bill they had passed had no teeth to it. She was so concerned, as her grandchildren were teenagers and she felt her time with them was so precious and important. She asked her uncle what she should do. Well she waited and she waited and weeks had gone by and he had not said anything. So she asked him again. He got a little upset with her. But a week later a bird had shown him the wisdom of her going to Washington, D.C. So she went and passed a strong bill for Freedom of Religion of Native Americans for this country. She was a true Lakota warrior and Bahá'í hero of our times. I remember my father-in-law, Pete Catches, a Lakota holy man, said if Patricia Locke and he were the two last Lakotas left, they could raise up a whole new Lakota Nation. And in many ways, I felt they have. (Lakota translates to "people of peace" in English. . . .)

There is so much that I could share. Life with her was rich with stories. But my most personal happened after she passed away. I had decided that I was going to write a curricula for the Lakota students for the prevention of alcohol / drugs and character education. I had read a book by Dr. Ghadirian on the subject and felt his spiritual concepts could easily be turned into Lakota concepts. One day I was riding to the town of Pierre with someone that was truly Pat's friend, Jacqueline Left Hand Bull. I told her what I had decided to do after much prayer and asked if she had any suggestions for me. She was quiet for some time. Then she said, "Cindy, Pat loved you very much, you should ask for her help." Then she shared a story of her calling on Pat's help with a real problem and how she had helped her. So I did, and boy my work took off! What I thought was going to take me two years, only took me a year. When I was almost done (always praying for Pat and Pete to help me each day), I called the superintendent of schools and low and behold she and some others were just writing a grant for character education and they ordered 1,600 books for four schools for the new school year and they committed to that for three years!

Later, Jacqueline told me, after my curriculum was in most of the schools, "Remember when you asked me if I had any suggestions? I thought, 'What can I tell Cindy? She can't write and she can't spell!'" But Jacqueline was a good friend and spiritually wise. She reached out and found exactly the help I needed. To make this story more wonderful, another friend, Alice Williams Quick, said, "Cindy, please let me edit your work!" She was very excited about it and was finishing a Ruhi study course with Bahá'ís and non-Bahá'ís, some of whom were teachers, and she knew my weakness in writing. She shared my project with them and they decided to take on my curriculum as a social / economic project and edited all my work! This project was a miracle. All of these successes were because of Pat, still continuing her work as a spiritual warrior. I know in my heart of hearts that this is true. She is still a miracle in my life.

Deb Chaplin

(Deb lived in Pierre, South Dakota and occasionally traveled to Wakpala to visit Patricia):

Although I spent a total of hours, not days, with Pat Locke, she inspired me to great hope and demonstrated the meaning of lasting dignity. Memory of her words and deeds, her inspiring spiritual presence, and the beauty of her countenance continue to be a major influence.

In the early 90s days, I worked in South Dakota state parks as the state naturalist / interpreter; involving developing exhibits in the best way possible for visitors' centers. Consultation with indigenous people of many tribes was a great benefit. Pat took particular interest in how plants were presented in exhibits; she asked that they be treated with great respect. This perspective proved unique and was invaluable input.

Pat was the first person to encourage me to explore energy healing. One beautiful day, again in the early 90s, she noticed some books in my home dealing with transformational energies; a light came into her eyes and she smiled and told me of how she was trained as a young girl to perceive energy fields. She taught me a specific technique for doing this without me having any idea how much this would set a lifelong pattern . . . much later, I was given the gift of learning energy healing through ancient Hawaiian traditions. Coming full circle, I had the privilege of working with this energy with Pat just six weeks before her death, in her tribal house on the Standing Rock Reservation—no air conditioning, internet, or cable . . . far away from a theater, mall, or multistoried building. Her dogs greeted me noisily in that dry, dusty land, and after being allowed entry past the canine guard, I encountered Kevin making her a simple piece of toast in their small kitchen. After our visit in her bed-sized, single windowed sick room, she reached up onto her shelf and gave me a small piece of pottery. This gift, so dear to me now, is certainly in itself a precious lesson from an audacious woman who taught, not only in classrooms, conference rooms, and international seminars, but also in her last days in her own humble home. She was and is an example and role model of the principles for which she lived and fought.

Juana C. Conrad

(Juana served on the National Spiritual Assembly with Patricia):

I first met Patricia when she was invited to a dinner during National Convention with her son, Mr. Kevin Locke. At that time, she had not yet embraced the Bahá'í Faith as her religion. I was struck from the moment I met her, by her dignity, intelligence and wisdom. Although I didn't know much about her, except that she was Kevin's mother, I found her fascinating. Shortly thereafter, I was invited by Kevin Locke to visit the Pine Ridge Sioux Reservation to give a talk to women about my recent trip to China with the organization, Women for International Peace and Arbitration, which had been holding seminars with Chinese women on various subjects of mutual interest. I accepted the invitation to go to the Reservation and Patricia Locke was one of the women present during my talk and slide show. She indicated she was moved by the talk, and presented me with an "eagle feather" wrapped in red cloth.

In a short span of time, she became a Bahá'í and thereafter was elected to the National Spiritual Assembly of the Bahá'ís of the United States and we became close friends. She became a member of Women for International Peace and Arbitration and participated in a WIPA delegation of educators to visit China at the invitation of the All China Women's Federation. The Chinese women were fascinated by the fact that she was a Native American and asked her many questions. Patricia remarked after the trip that she found American women and the Chinese women had much in common.

I was fortunate enough to be considered a friend of Patricia. She explained to me that in her culture, the older women would mentor the younger ones, and she believed it was her role to help the women on the Assembly who were younger than she was. I received a few tips from her and gratefully accepted them as being from a woman I greatly admired.

She was generous of spirit. She would shower gifts upon her friends. On occasion, I would admire a pin, ring, or bracelet on other women and each time, the woman would say, "Patricia Locke gave it to me." I was also a recipient of her generosity.

She loved, and was so proud of, her children and grandchildren. She moved back to the Reservation from city life because she wanted to be near her grandchildren and influence their lives. In talking about Reservation life, she said she didn't like to visit areas of the country where she couldn't see the horizon, which she characterized as "horizon deprivation."

There was a shift of consciousness on the National Assembly when Patricia spoke of the philosophy of the Lakota people as it pertains to children and youth, who are always included with the adults in all events, and never separated. She explained that when the National Assembly has conferences, meetings, and other events, the children and youth should be with the adults and not be separated into separate rooms. This had a profound impact on our thinking and actions.

During consultation at the meetings of the National Assembly, occasionally Patricia would . . . begin consultation by telling a joke, to be sure she had everyone's attention. One day, I said to her, "Pat, I am on to you. I know what you are doing." She smiled sheepishly and said, "don't tell the others."

She had a wonderful sense of humor. I fondly remember her telling the members of the National Assembly stories of her experiences while traveling to other countries, after which we collapsed in laughter as she was a great storyteller.

My only wish is that each reader (of this biography) would have had the privilege of knowing Patricia as a friend and colleague. It was truly a priceless experience and one for which I will forever be grateful.

Linda S. Covey

(This in an excerpt of an email to Kevin. Linda currently teaches psychology at Missouri State University's College of International Business at Liaoning Normal University, Dalian, China.)

(I have a treasured memory of when) I met your mother and had lunch with her. It was at the national convention that year the NSA had it in a big hotel in Skokie, IL, so that more of the friends could attend. It was my first time to attend convention, and I specifically wanted to ask some questions about how to deal with my nativeness and the Faith—(I) was really struggling with those issues, feeling like I had one foot in one world and one foot in the other world. I had been passed the Pipe (shortly) . . . before that convention, and my whole world had blown apart in the process. Your mother helped me immensely at our lunch. . . . After listening patiently to my story, with just a sentence or two, she answered my questions of dividedness and eased my troubled heart. After lunch, your mother took me shoe shopping with her—I'll never forget it—can see clearly in my mind's eye our looking at shoes for her together, and she commenting on what kind of shoes she liked and why. I followed her in spirit and prayer as she went through the agony of her later illnesses, losing both legs. Shopping for shoes became deeply meaningful.

When the NSA produced a memorial tape of her and gave it to the delegates at the following convention, our delegate from Missouri gave that tape to me. I have greatly treasured it and the stories your mother tells on that tape of her travels, especially in relation to the wind blowing across her face. . . .

One time in particular comes to mind when I had just finished watching the tape, again, for inspiration, and then an email came immediately from Cindy (Catches). . . . We talked about this wind your mother mentioned and I shared with Cindy (when) a strange, extremely strong wind visited me on Bear Butte, the one time I spent a night on that sacred mountain. It blew from all four directions! Cindy gave me an answer to that wind without my even needing to ask it, but it came up in the first place because of the wind your mother mentions in that most precious memorial tape of her.

Carol Curtis
(This remembrance of Patricia was addressed to Kevin Locke. Carol first met Patricia when Patricia traveled to Majuro in the Pacific):

As you remember Majuro is an atoll, which is a string of very small islands and reefs that string around a lagoon, so one is never very far from the ocean. Well, your mother stated to Counselor Betra Majmeto and me that she wanted to visit the beach. So we decided to take her to Laura, end of the road, to let her enjoy the ocean. We needed to get some food, so we stopped and got peanut butter, jam, bread, and I think some fruit. I picked up my children, around maybe seven and nine years old at the time, and headed out in my very old Izuzu Trooper, which had only two doors and two windows that worked.

So we got to the airport terminal area and there was a roadblock because they were working on the road. Before I had a chance to explain to Patricia that they never stop us for long . . . she looked at me in frustration and I think some anger, and exclaimed: "YOU SHOULD HAVE TAKEN ANOTHER ROAD!"

Well, with this proclamation I looked at Betra in the rearview mirror, and she was stifling a laugh with her hand, as I was. After your mother gave me a chance to say something, I said. . .

"Patricia, you see the lagoon on your right (all of three feet away), and you see across the runway, and the big rocks on the other side, well on the other side of the rocks is the ocean, in other words, there is no other road to take!"

By this time they had let us drive on . . . and your mother's expression was one of total dumbfoundedness (she was brilliant), but in this case she was literally speechless . . . and she said, "OH!!!!!!"

Then we proceeded to Laura and the beautiful beaches there and we had a fun time in the water and she especially enjoyed playing with my children. We took some photos of her with my children, which she probably had somewhere when she returned. We ate lots of peanut butter, jam, and bread, which your mother loved.

She probably told you how difficult it was to get her on the plane out of Majuro since the plane was so overbooked. If it hadn't been for Behin White, who can be very persistent, your mother might still be there until now.

I was lucky to be able to spend a fair amount of time with Patricia, because I kept running into her wherever I went in town . . . even though I was teaching at the high school, and very busy. It was a great privilege to get to know her and to be with her for a few days . . . and every time I think about her, I laugh, thinking about our ride to Laura.

Incidentally I know you met Betra; she is the first Bahá'í of the Marshall Islands, the first woman Bahá'í of all of Micronesia (not including Kiribati), the first indigenous ABM,* and the first indigenous Counselor in Micronesia. A very remarkable woman who never was able to attend high school, and became a teacher at the age of fourteen. Betra passed away on December 17, 2008 after a very long and wonderfully interesting life.

Mary Lee Johns

(This was in a letter addressed to Kevin. Mary first met Patricia in a Native Studies program at San Francisco State in 1969. They developed a close and enduring friendship and often shared speaking platforms):

We have always wanted to know what actually happened to your mother. The last time I saw her was when she came to Lincoln to participate in the International Family Conference. Both she and I were speakers. She looked so frail and sad, my heart really went out to her, but when she spoke it was the same person I knew for years. If you could someday share the information with our family we would appreciate it.

I don't know if you knew this but I first met your mother back in 1969 when she came to lecture at San Francisco State. I was involved in getting the first Native Studies Program started at State, along with Richard Oaks and others. Bea Medicine was head of it and she brought your mother in as well as Vine Deloria and other excellent leaders. I was so impressed with her, and was hooked from that point on. Not only was she physically beautiful, but she was so intelligent and she dressed so fantastic. I have for years used her and my Aunt

---

* An ABM, Auxiliary Board Member, is an individual appointed by the Counselors to serve as assistants to the Counselor. The appointments are usually for five-year terms and the individuals cannot serve on Bahá'í administrative institutions while they are serving as Auxiliary Board Members.

Eunice as role models. She gave so much of herself—if we only had that type of dedication in the younger people who are in leadership today, we would be so much better off.

Jack McCants

(Jack served on the National Spiritual Assembly with Patricia):

Pat and I were assigned by our NSA (National Spiritual Assembly) to go to Haifa to represent the United States at the funeral of Rúhíyyih Khánum. Pat felt that the Bahá'í world had lost its greatest defender of the Native folk in the world today.

She was unique. None of us had ever really heard of her when she was elected to our NSA. She was God's choice to be sure. She spoke up strongly on issues, and was most gifted in wrapping her presentations in humor and Indian Native stories. While in Haifa, the House of Justice was consulting with our NSA on a very serious and sensitive topic. We, as a body, had been asked to wait in a separate conference room while they considered the subject. Everyone was uptight and extremely tense. Pat looked us all over and stated, "This is really a Maalox moment" (from) the prevalent TV commercial at that time. It brought the necessary laughter and needed relaxation of our souls while we waited to meet again with the House of Justice to get their decision on the matter at hand. It became a repeated "inside joke."

I loved Pat because she was honest. She was just. She spoke her mind and shared freely her thoughts, her experiences from her many trips, her long eventful life, and she was always deeply aware of what others were feeling. She was not a "yes man," "rubberstamp" of other's thoughts, but almost always had a creative contribution to make of her own.

She wanted to be called an "Indian." She did not want to be called a "Native American." She said Eskimos, Hawaiians, and others were all lumped together as "Native Americans." She was proud to be who she was . . . an American Indian. I cannot think of Pat without tears of love and happiness coming into my heart. I could talk to her heart-to-heart, nothing held back . . . we were one in the spirit of this Faith, and everywhere I was with her, whether in this country or somewhere else, that never changed. No fake . . . no put-on . . . just happy to be alive together in this wonderful world of reality that we both called home . . . the Faith of Bahá'u'lláh.

She was like a flaming star . . . bringing her light to the entire world and vanishing into God's embrace, which to us is darkness but, to her, bliss upon bliss, I am quite sure.

Carol Miller

(Carol and Patricia were frequently at events together. Carol was involved with the Martin Luther King Day activities in Atlanta and arranged for Patricia's participation):

I just had an amazing dream of Pat.

We were in a fairgrounds, and part of a contest. We were judging the winner. We spent a long time debating, analyzing, and measuring what ribbons were the longest. There were two ribbons that stretched for meters. One was blue and one was red. Pat was in a state of great emotion and consternation. When we finished measuring which ribbon was the longest . . . to determine the winner, she emphatically stated that it was not important; that the only thing that was important now was TEACHING THE FAITH to the Indian people.

Then the dream ended. She was very vehement, concerned and emphatic. It felt like an urgent message.

Raymond Morrison

(Raymond Lives in Mobridge, South Dakota, and was a great admirer of Patricia):

I first met Pat Locke in the late 1980s. I found her to be a pleasant-looking, serene woman who could calm almost any situation, no matter how agitated it might be. But when she was upset by something, the change in her personality from Ghandi-like calm to slight perturbation was as great as most of us going from normal to total frenzy. And people respected that.

I talked to her several times at her daughter, Winona's, where she stayed. May, Winona's oldest, was pretty much raised, but the two boys, Pawna (also known as Hepana) and Duta, were still little boys. Pat was a wise woman who had many creative, innovative ideas about the world, but watching her interact in Winona's household with those boys probably gave me just as much enjoyment. She loved those boys completely. When Pawna got into a car accident, Pat died shortly afterwards of a broken heart.

I also am proud that I got to know Pat before she started getting her richly deserved financial awards. As a writer living on a writer's wages, she knew the ins and outs of making-do. One of my favorite memories of her was when she told me about a copy machine in Mobridge where you could get two copies for the price of one because of the way the machine was set up.

Pat was a friend to my mother. She was a friend to me. When I decided to go back to graduate school she bought some huge steaks and we went out to the river where we had a great picnic dinner.

Pat was a true Bahá'í. She was a friend to all.

Dorothy Nelson

(Dorothy served on the National Spiritual Assembly with Patricia):

When I think of Patricia, I love to remember the ancient Anishinabe Indian poem about the young girl who learned to communicate with her spirit guide and began her journey of life. She became a woman and set her foot on the path of motherhood. When she died, her children said: "You will always walk with us, Mother, even when you cross the river to the valley on the other side." The children watched her as she went alone to the beautifully lit valley and as the beauty of the light embraced her, they said: "We cannot see her, but she is with us. A mother like ours is more than a memory; she is a living presence."

Patricia is and has been a living presence in my life since I first sent her a book about Indian law before she was a Bahá'í. Kevin had told me that Patricia was a dedicated defender of Indian sovereignty, education, and religious freedom. When she became a member of the National Spiritual Assembly in 1993 and one of the closest, dearest friends I have ever had, we had exciting and stimulating conversations about these matters. So, when I was invited to give the Clara and Hyde Dunn lecture in Sydney, Australia in 1996 and then to visit Auckland, New Zealand, I asked my hosts to arrange visits with the Maoris of New Zealand and the aboriginal peoples of Australia. I had prepared a brief talk on Indian sovereignty and was absolutely surprised in each instance to walk into a room to a standing ovation with the Native people waving copies of a decision of mine. It was State of Alaska v. Native village of Venetie Tribal Government in which I had upheld the sovereign right of the Native village to impose business taxes. Patricia had e-mailed a copy of my opinion to them. The fact that it was later reversed by the United States Supreme Court did not diminish the love fest that I had with these people during my stay.

What was most amazing to me about Patricia was that when she became a Bahá'í, she transformed herself as an advocate for human rights for Indians to an advocate for human rights for all peoples. She also changed her mode of advocating needed change from an adversarial mode to one of a consultative mode.

Patricia gave me an Indian cover for my prayer book, which I carry to each and every meeting of the National Spiritual Assembly. As the Anishinabe children said: "We cannot see her, but she is with us . . . she is a living presence."

Rhonda Palmer

(Rhonda is a nurse who attended to Rúhíyyih Khánum during her final illness. She had never met Patricia, but in a dream she felt that Rúhíyyih Khánum asked her to take care of Patricia, so she volunteered her services):

Life has so many ways of giving us problems. Being born hurts. Childhood is full of injury. Living and suffering go hand in hand. Her life (Patricia's) had a sorrow from the beginning that had nothing to do with the pain of the body. Her people were sad and had lost their words. She found around her a world that could not see her or her children or her people. With characteristic courage she helped to reclaim an entire language and lived as a teacher of life to those who had the honor to be near her. She took her sorrow and made it a road to faithfulness.

Illness tried to take away her dignity but she had too much strength to let it win. I stayed with her for a few precious nights in the hospital at the end of her life. She would wake up and try to make sense out of what was happening. "Why are you here?" she would ask repeatedly. Finally I told the simple truth: I was a nurse, and had been impelled to offer my services because of a dream in which Rúhíyyih Khánum had told me to come. She smiled and nodded at that, and was able to sleep.

Later she woke up and asked for her purse. She fished around in it for a while and then handed me a small, woven bag, probably from Guatemala. "This is for you," she said. I later learned that her generosity was legend, and that there were many around the world who treasured the gifts she had given them.

Shelly Rastal

(Shelly was one of Patricia's friends):

When a soul like Patricia Locke is brought into the world, it is like a piece of heaven is among us, a soul who carries the light, and the divine music. Now more than ever, we need Patricia's spirit to remember that reality is love. Her love was the cornerstone of everything she ever did, from caring for her seven dogs to serving on the National Spiritual Assembly. . . .

Janet Rubenstein

(Janet was an executive secretary for the National Spiritual Assembly and knew Patricia through that function):

Patricia was very private. She exemplified for me how a woman should behave. She was the epitome of decorum, discipline, sensitivity, and genuine kindness and humility. Her great joy with simple gifts given to her, whether physical or service, gave the donor a feeling of wonderful accomplishment.

I loved her and always will. I only hope that I can bring happiness to others in the way she did.

Joanne Shenandoah:

(Joanne is a popular singer / performer from the Iroquois Confederacy in New York. She and Patricia served on a variety of American Indian projects together.)

In 1999, the eve of the Millennium, I was asked to accompany my husband Doug George Kanentiio to attend the Congress of the Parliament of the World's Religions in Cape Town, South Africa. Interesting how sometimes in life your journey takes you far and wide to unveil the dynamics of history and marvelous, personal and life-changing experiences. How blessed! We were part of a large indigenous delegation to the Parliament; among our group were Apaches, Pawnees, Navajos, and the Lakota family of Patricia and Kevin Locke.

I was asked to sing at the opening of the Parliament, an unanticipated honor, which affected me spiritually and emotionally. I didn't comprehend the effect of the song I selected would have on the 6,000 delegates gathered in the former apartheid state. When I entered the assembly hall I saw a sea of delegates dressed in their distinctive clothing. I had sung the Prophecy song previously but in Cape Town I felt the need to ask my ancestors to give me a part of their strength and knowledge so the music would flow in a way to effect true peace. Before me were imams, priests, nuns, monks, scholars, activists, politicians, and indigenous leaders from all directions of the earth. I was amazed but could feel the power of the moment as the room became silent when I sung: "Awaken, stand up and be counted. We are being recognized in the spirit world. We are responsible for ourselves, our families and our nations."

One of the most memorable experiences of my life was the opportunity to have a personal tour of the prison at Roben Island by Ahmed Kathrada, who was confined in a cell next to Nelson Mandela for over two decades. We walked through the prison with Dr. Huston Smith, Phil Cousineau, and Gary Rhine (filmmakers), who were making a documentary about our journey to Africa. As we toured the facility I thought of our own people, oppressed in North America, with many of our own people confined because of their political and spiritual beliefs.

I was thrilled to hear that Kevin Locke (Lakota dancer and musician) and his mother Patricia were going to join our group, as I had the wonderful opportunity to be able to work with Kevin a number of times throughout the years. When I met Kevin's mother, Pat, I was taken by her striking appearance and straightforward manner. She was unassuming and very kind to me. We had a number of opportunities to spend time together during the conference and at various social events. At one dinner I recall how she loved "prawns." I am a vegetarian and found her menu selection intriguing, her table conversation stimulating. She was determined to sample the local cuisine in all of its diversity. The entire evening was full of celebration as Pat and I joined the local African women by sitting on the floor and keeping rhythm as we joined in their festive and joyous display of traditional music and dance. I learned later that Pat had been a hula dancer in California during World War II.

One evening she took me aside to talk to me privately. She said that she was particularly impressed with the message of peace, which I expressed in song during my concerts and wanted to thank me. As a result of my music she said she was determined to lay aside all hard feelings she had towards people who may have had wronged her in the past. I was moved by her sincerity and told her it is not easy to forgive, but that it was necessary to free the soul.

Through my concert, Pat learned of one of our prophets, Hiawatha, who had lost all his daughters, murdered by an evil chief named Tadadaho. Hiawatha was so grieved that he wandered aimlessly for many days until he arrived at a small lake. His sadness was so overwhelming that it alarmed a flock of ducks. They rose into the sky taking all the water with them. On the bed of the lake he saw beautiful shells, which he wove into a string. He realized that someone could lift their grief if they were to hold the shells and say the right words of condolence. At that moment the Peacemaker appeared and spoke the healing words to Hiawatha, restoring him to sanity. Hiawatha then joined the Peacemaker as they formed the Haudenosaunee Confederacy, a league of democratic nations who adhere to the Great Law of Peace. A united Iroquois delegation went to confront Tadadaho, who, in the face of this unity, acknowledged his evil ways, abandoned sorcery, and embraced the Great Law. Hiawatha forgave Tadadaho; we could do no less.

Pat grabbed both of my hands and said a very heartfelt "thank you," then placed in my hand a small beautiful gold ring with a Native person carved on the front. She said, "I want you to have this; it belonged to my mother, now I know it belongs to you."

I put on the ring every now and then. When I place it on my finger I recall Pat's words and how important it is that I continue singing these songs of peace. We all have our respective duties on this earth as well as individual talents. If we live life as a celebration, as Pat did, the world will be a happier place. It was not long after our trip to Africa that I had heard Pat had passed to the spirit world. I'm certain when she took her journey along the path of stars her ancestors were there to greet her. Her spirit was powerful and good, leaving an indelible impression on me for which I shall be always grateful.

David Grant

(David is from Scotland, and was circumnavigating the globe via a horsedrawn cart when he first met Patricia in Mongolia. Kevin said he came to Mobridge in the winter of 1996–97 and "wound up spending the worst winter since the ice age"):

I first met Pat Locke in a concert hall in Ulaanbaatar (Mongolia). She was with her son Kevin and granddaughter Kimimila, who were performing traditional Lakota flute music and dances. This was their last stop on a tour that had begun in Siberia, before returning to the United States. I was present with my family because we happened to be wintering in Ulaanbaatar, a way-stop along the road on our seven-year-long journey around the world by horsedrawn caravan.

What I really remember is a marvelously hospitable, friendly, warm, and loving human being. My only sorrow is that, at least while still inhabiting this earth, I shall never again be able to sit and chat with her in her kitchen, with a dog or three around our feet.

Epilogue

Patricia's remarkable life appears even more awesome in light of the part she played in the seachanges humanity has been going through since the middle of the 1800s. Climate change, technological advances, rampant crime and corruption, improved rights for minorities and women, species extinction, increased life expectancies, globalization, wars and rumors of wars, scientific advances, depletion of natural resource, improved literacy, reduced infant mortality, domestic violence, marked reduction in prejudice, increase of substance abuse, and the Internet are all parts of an endless list. There have been more changes, for better and for worse, than during the preceding thousands of years.

Two processes can be seen as causing these changes. One is destructive and the other is constructive. Bahá'u'lláh's statement, "*Soon will the present-day order be rolled up, and a new one spread out in its stead,*"[104] reflects both, eloquently describing this age of transition. Patricia played a significant role in the most beneficial changes.

From at least the time of the tower of Babel[105] people have lived in groups separated from one another by language and geography. With this isolation, each group developed its own traditions and characteristics. The time is ripe for each group to bring the contributions from its unique history to humanity's banquet table.

The coming together is a long process that has taken place in many ways. People have gone from the nomadic life to being hunters and gatherers, to agriculture, to the industrial age, and more recently, to the digital age. More and more people are leaving their ancestral lands for urban living. As they leave their remote, homogeneous, and isolated living for large, concentrated areas, a mixture of people of various ethnic backgrounds has resulted. The earth is increasingly becoming interrelated. As Bahá'u'lláh said, *"the earth is one country, and mankind its citizens."*[106]

However, there are many who have not benefited from these changes. The gap between those who have gained from the decades of change and those who have been marginalized is graphically pictured where sprawling shantytowns—without plumbing or electricity—spring up next to ultramodern metropolitan airports.

The Bahá'í writings have much to say about these different groups and the importance of coming together and meeting the challenges of unequal benefits. Of special interest for Patricia's life is what has been said about American Indians. In at least two important instances 'Abdu'l-Bahá mentioned American Indians directly. *Some Answered Questions* is a book that records the answers to a variety of questions regarding Bahá'í teachings that 'Abdu'l-Bahá gave during table conversations. In it he said that in comparison to the Arabs, the *"Indians of America were as advanced as a Plato."*[107]* Chapters II & III, describing Patricia's background and Lakota traditions, certainly fit with this view of American Indians.

In another book, *Tablets of the Divine Plan,* 'Abdu'l-Bahá says: "Attach great importance to the indigenous population of America. For these souls may be likened unto the ancient inhabitants of the Arabian Peninsula, who, prior to the Mission of Muḥammad, were like unto savages. When the light of Muḥammad shone forth in their midst, however, they became so radiant as to illumine the world. Likewise, these Indians, should they be educated and guided, there can be no doubt that they will become so illumined as to enlighten the whole world."[108]

---

* Plato, a Greek philosopher, 427–347B.C.E. His best-known work, *The Republic*, outlines the features of an ideal civilization.

If the Arab world, which was at such a low point, could progress to make the enormous contributions to civilization that it did,* how much more might be expected from the education of American Indians, who, according to 'Abdu'l-Bahá, were already at the level of a Plato?

Two conditions are implied in the above quoted passage. First is the importance of reaching indigenous people. The second has to do with education and guidance.

It is unlikely that 'Abdu'l-Bahá had in mind any current educational system or standard. His educational model, while placing character development above intellectual training, includes a balance among spiritual, moral, intellectual, and physical education. This is not to be found in today's schools. His vision of both education and guidance seems closer to the education reflected in Patricia's heritage than today's norms.

Concerning illumination, 'Abdu'l-Bahá spoke of two kinds of light. Beyond the physical, there is intellectual illumination. He said, "The light of the intellect enables us to understand and realize all that exists, but it is only the Divine Light that can give us sight for the invisible things, and which enables us to see truths that will only be visible to the world thousands of years hence. . . . Thus it is this Light which we must strive to seek, for it is greater than any other."[109]

The promised enlightenment goes beyond seeing things more clearly and having better insight. It opens up new and undreamed of worlds with an unimaginable scope in which all can benefit from human resourcefulness.

The big question is how to do this. The path to be followed for these blessings is found in attaching importance to the process that 'Abdu'l-Bahá mentioned. There are no detailed instructions. The

---

* For example, see Cobb, Stanwood, *Islamic Contribution to Civilization.* Washington, DC: Avalon Press, 1963.

challenge, which is also a bounty, is both figuring out what needs to be done and then doing it.

In a letter written on behalf of Shoghi Effendi to the National Spiritual Assembly of Central America and Mexico is found this statement regarding Indians:

> As you know, the Master attached the utmost importance to the teaching of the Indians in America. . . .
>
> If the light of Divine Guidance enters properly into the lives of the Indians, it will be found that they will arise with a great power and will become an example of spirituality and culture to all of the people in these countries.[110]

While the world is a long way from understanding the full impact of these comments, they are not to be taken lightly. In the past there have been many attempts to reach American Indians. Some have proved effective and some have not. Some have started well, but have been abandoned. Too often, attempts to reach American Indians have been on the terms, and from the perspective of, the dominant culture.

On an individual level there have been a great number of remarkable American Indian Bahá'ís, including Patricia, whose impact on human progress have truly been illuminating. Even before becoming a Bahá'í, she was sensitive to the spirit of this age in her efforts to educate her people.

Ferris Paisano, a Nez Percé Indian, sees partial fulfillment of those promises with the institute process and the Ruhi series. These include study courses and a series of workbooks that were developed for the purpose of educating Indians in South America who had become Bahá'ís. They proved effective, were further developed, and are now used all over the world, illuminating many and diverse people in many lands and languages. They are certainly helping to *enlighten the whole world.*

Another consideration has to do with perspective. Looking through a window from one side of the street, a person can see certain things.

Looking from the other side, different things are seen. What is viewed from each side appears different from the other. There is a human tendency to assume whatever we, personally, see or understand is what the world is really like. Many people are suspicious or contemptuous of other perspectives. History has shown that far too often blood has been spilled when someone expresses a view from a different perspective.

In *Tablets of the Divine Plan*, 'Abdu'l-Bahá advised Bahá'ís going to different countries to learn the language spoken in that county.[111] That idea can be applied to all means of communicating. It involves reaching out in a means suitable to the hearer. It is a genuine desire to connect, heart-to-heart, and to have a caring interest in the concerns of others.

Patricia understood the different perspectives people had and the need to speak in a way others can understand. There are countless examples in her life when she shared the Lakota understanding in a way that would enlighten rather than antagonize. For example, her articles in the *Mobridge Tribune* give details of many different perceptions that people of different groups have. She always addressed people in ways that would fit into their view of life, and their perspective and understanding. Her life was an outstanding example of striving toward 'Abdu'l-Bahá's vision through a practical application of His mandate to give great importance to indigenous peoples. Her life was ample evidence that success will be neither easy nor smooth. It was a continuous example of learning from setbacks, focusing, not on the difficulties encountered, but on the goals to be won and carrying forth with love, energy, and persistence for the blessing and illumination of the whole world.

What would the world be like if more people followed her lead?

Glossary of Lakota Words

One of Patricia's passions was the preservation of Indian languages. For this reason, Lakota words that are important to her life story are included in this glossary. In 2008 the Lakota Language Consortium published the *New Lakota Dictionary* that is the most up-to-date and comprehensive reference for the Lakota language. That is the basis for the following words.

English Words	Lakota	Approximate meaning
becoming a woman	išnáthi awíčhalowaŋpi	This sacred rite for girls attaining adulthood consists of older, highly respected women going into a tent with the younger woman explaining what it means to be a Lakota woman.
bravery	wóohitika	One of the four main Lakota values.
child	wakȟáŋheža	A sacred being.
chippewa	ȟaȟátȟuŋwaŋ	Also known as Anishinabe and Ojibway.
compassionate woman	tȟawáčhiŋ wašté wíŋ	Name given to Patricia Locke.
courage	wóčhaŋtet'iŋze	One of the four main Lakota values.
Dakota	Dakȟóta	Friend or ally, a member of one of the eastern Dakota tribes.
Gate Keeper	Thiyópa awáŋyaŋke	The one who meets the soul after death, asks its name, and decides if the soul is to proceed on the spirit path or head to oblivion.
Creator/ Creations	Wakȟáŋ Tȟáŋka	Can refer to either the Great Spirit or to all creation, depending on usage. This should not be confused with pantheism.
generosity	wówačhaŋtognaka	One of the four main Lakota values.
Great Spirit	Wakȟáŋ Tȟáŋka	A reference to the Creator or God.

give away	wíȟpeya	To give things away; takes place on notable occasions such as a year after a death.
Grandfather	Tȟuŋkášila	While this is used for a biological grandfather, it has other connotations. White Buffalo Calf Maiden explained that Tȟuŋkášila had sent her. Spiritually, it is a reference to the Great Spirit.
grandmother	uŋčí	Grandmother—a term Patricia preferred for herself.
harmony	wólakȟota	A core Lakota principle. In prayer or in a sacred/non secular context this word implies a divine condition of peace, harmony, unity, balance, order, etc.
The Hawk that Hunts While Walking	Čhetáŋ Wakhúwa Máni	One of the names of Patricia's maternal great grandfather.
His Red Nation	Tȟaóyate Dúta	One of the names of Patricia's maternal great grandfather.
Hunkpapa	Húŋkpapȟa	One of seven Lakota tribes. Patricia was registered as Húŋkpapȟa through her mother.
first to arise	Tȟokéya inažiŋ	Kevin Locke's Lakota name.
Lakota	Lakȟóta	Friend or ally, a member of one of the western Dakota tribes.

Little Crow	Kȟaŋǧí Čík'ala	Patricia's maternal great grandfather. It was probably an incorrect translation and application of his father's name, Čhetáŋ Wakhúwa Máni
making a relative	iyáčhiŋ	A ritual of adoption for someone who has lost a loved one.
my relations	mitákuye oyás'iŋ	This conveys the idea that everything in this world is a physical reflection of spiritual reality, affirming the interrelationship of all things.
Nakota	Hóhe	Lakota name for the Assiniboine tribe.
pow-wow	wačhípi	A gathering to dance, sing, socialize, and honor American Indian culture.
purification	iníkaǧa	Sweat Lodge—ceremony for purification.
release of the soul	wanáǧi yuškápi	A ceremony one year after a person dies that releases the soul to the spirit world.
respect	ohóla	One of the four main Lakota values, especially for older relatives.
Sioux	Sioux	Of either Chippewa or Algonquin origin including both Dakota and Lakota. Considered pejorative by many members because the Chippewa meaning connotes a sneaky, cunning snake.

sun dance	wiwáŋyaŋg wačhípi	A sacred ritual dance: Literally, "They Dance Gazing At The Sun."
Teton	Thítȟuŋwaŋ	Archaic name for all seven Lakota tribes.
tossing the ball	thápa waŋkáyeyapi	A game and also a spiritual rite. A ball is thrown in a certain direction. Whoever catches it is responsible for the creatures and environment in that area.
vision quest	haŋbléčheyapi	A ritual for young men to seek guidance for their lives.
warrior	akíčhita	Camp police; on duty for all tribal services.
warrior society	okȟólakičhiye	A social welfare group that devote their lives to taking care of the sick, elderly, and infirm and providing the protection and needs of the tribe.
White Buffalo Calf Woman	Ptesáŋwiŋ	Believed to be a Messenger from God for the Lakota people.
wisdom	wóksape	One of the four main Lakota values—a life-long quest.

BRIEF GUIDE TO PRONUNCIATION

There had been no written form of the Lakota language until missionaries desired to translate the Bible. Over time, the number of letters was expanded and phonemes were included to assist readers with pronounciation. According to the *New Lakota Dictionary* (compiled by Jan Ullrich and published by the Lakota Language Consortium, Bloomington, 2008) there are five oral vowels in Lakota and three nasal vowels that were added to the standard English alphabet. The language is also rich in diphthongs and glottal stops. There are many sounds for which there is no direct English equivalent. The chart below approximates some of the sounds of Lakota phonation. See http://www.lakhota.org/ALPHABET/alphabet.htm for guide to Lakota phonemes.

Lakota symbol	Approximate pronunciation
a	like *a* in *father*
e	like *e* in *bed*
i	like *i* in *sit*
o	somewhat like *a* in *sofa*
u	like *oo* in *boot*
aŋ	like *o* in *monkey*, nasalized
iŋ	like *i* in *mint*, nasalized
uŋ	somewhat like *oo* in *moon*, nasalized; no exact English example
g	like *g* in *got*, but not like *g* in *gin*
ğ	like the northern French *r* (as in *Paris*), no exact English equivalent
h	like *h* in *hat*
ȟ	close to the Spanish *x* in *Mexico*, but with more guttural friction
č	almost like *ch* in *rich* (unaspirated), but not like *g* in *gin*
čh	like *ch* in *chin* (aspirated)
č'	like *c* but followed by a glottal stop
k	like *k* in *skip*, but not like *k* in *kip* or like *g* in *gig*
kh	like *k* in *kiss* (aspirated k)
kȟ	no equivalent in English, connects *k* and *ȟ*
k'	like *k* but followed by a glottal stop
p	like *p* in *spin* or in *happy*, not like *p* in *pin* or *b* in *bin*
ph	like *p* in *pin* (aspirated *p*)
pȟ	no equivalent in English
p'	like *p* but followed by a glottal stop

t	like *t* in *still,* but not like *t* in *till* or like *d* in *dill*
th	like *t* in *tip* (aspirated *t*)
tȟ	no equivalent in English
t'	like *t* but followed by a glottal stop
s	like *s* in *so*
š	like *sh* in *shop*
z	like *z* in *zero*
ž	like *s* in *pleasure*
b	like *b* in *boy*
l	like *l* in *lamp*
m	like *m* in *map*
n	like *n* in *nap*
w	like *w* in *was*
y	Like *y* in *yes*
'	catch in the throat, like the pause between the syllables in *uh-oh*

Interviewees

Grateful appreciation is expressed for the following people, who allowed the author to interview them, and who consented to have their remarks included:

Atkinson, Larry
Atkinson, Robert
Claymore, Duane
Davidson, Art
Eakan, Maynard
Emerson, Gloria
End of Horn, Austin
End of Horn, Robert, Jr.
End of Horn, Robert Sr.
End of Horn, Stoney
Flying Earth, Winona
Goodhouse, Sharon
Greene, Harlene
Hall, Jo
Henrikson, Gerald
Kimble, Gary
Left Hand Bull, Jacqueline
Locke, Dorothy
Locke, Kevin
Locke, Kimimila
Locke, Winona

Locke, Waniya
Medicine, Earl
McCants, Jack
Milligan, Frances
Makepeace, Frances
Makepeace, Sean
McKnight, Sheridan
Napoleon, Harold
Nelson, Dorothy
Nelson, James
Pease, Janine Windy Boy
Real Bird, Lanny
Richardson, Edwin
Stein, Wayne
Taken Alive, Dolores
Taken Alive, Imogene
Tiger, Debora
Walters, Ron
Vermillion, Laurel
Yarlott, David

NOTES

1. Robert Henderson, from a recording of the memorial service for Patricia Locke.

2. See: http://www.state.sd.us/oia/standing.asp.

3. Patricia Locke, from a documentary on her life filmed in 1991.

4. Frances Milligan, recorded interview with the author, June, 18, 2007.

5. Ibid.

6. Jacqueline Left Hand Bull, recorded interview with the author, July 13, 2007.

7. Kevin Locke, recorded interview, July 21, 2008.

8. Patricia Locke, from a recorded talk given at Southern Maine University in the early 1990s.

9. The background for this chapter was drawn from a documentary Patricia made in 1990 as well as conversations with various family members and information gleaned from the Internet.

10. Dan Roberts, "A Moment in Time," radio series, University of Richmond.

11. Little Crow (as recalled by his son), quoted in Dee Brown, *Bury My Heart at Wounded Knee,* p. 44

12. Richard Dillon, *North American Indian Wars,* p. 126.

13. Ward Churchill, *Kill the Indian, Save the Man: The Genocidal Impact of American Indian Residential Schools* (City Lights Publishers, 2004) traces the history of removing Native American children from their homes to residential schools (in Canada) or Indian boarding schools (in the U.S.A.) as part of government policies of the 1880s–1980s, which the author views as genocidal. The book is titled after the stated objective of the government program, as articulated by Richard Henry Pratt, the architect of the U.S. system.

14. A great deal of information is available online about White Buffalo Calf Woman. Also see James R. Walker, *Lakota Belief and Ritual,* University

of Nebraska Press and Bison Books, 1991; William K. Powers, *Ogalala Religion*, University of Nebraska Press, 1975, 1977.

15. Patricia Locke, *The Maine Scholar*, p. 207.

16. There are many fine references explaining the seven rites. John Neihardt recorded Black Elk's comprehensive understanding of them in *Black Elk Speaks*.

17. The original version of this story is in Ella Deloria's classic, *Speaking of Indians*.

18. Janet Rubenstein, letter to Kevin Locke.

19. Kevin Locke, recorded interview with the author, February 21, 2008.

20. Frances Makepeace, recorded interview with the author, August 31, 2007.

21. Winona Flying Earth, recorded interview with the author, August 7, 2007.

22. Jacqueline Left Hand Bull, recorded interview with the author, July 13, 2007.

23. Maynard Eakan, recorded interview with the author, July 10, 2008.

24. In addition to being a successful businessman, Art is a world acclaimed mountaineer, naturalist, adventurer, writer, and photographer. Twice he climbed Mt. McKinley—North America's highest peak. Art much prefers the Athabascan name for this mountain, Denali, meaning the *Great One*. His first climb was in 1985 and he was the only westerner in an otherwise all-Japanese party. Later, he was part of the first winter ascent. His book, *Minus 148°*, describes that climb. It is still sold in the Denali National Park in Alaska. After the *Exxon Valdez* oil spill on March 24, 1989, he was commissioned to write *In the Wake of Exxon Valdez* explaining its impact. Other books include *Edge of the Earth: Crown of the Sky*, illustrated by Art Wolf; *Light on the Land*, a creation anthology, *On Thin Ice*, about the Arctic Wildlife Refuge; and *Alakshak: The Great Land*, essays about Alaska, with illustrations by Art Wolf.

25. Art Davidson: This and all subsequent quotations from him, as well as much of the information in this chapter, were from a recorded interview with the author in Anchorage on May 28, 2008.

26. Harold Napoleon, interview with the author, April 2009.

27. Duane Claymore, recorded interview with the author, April 4, 2009.

28. Janine Pease-Windy Boy, "The Tribally Controlled Community Colleges Act of 1978: An Expansion of Federal Indian Trust Responsibility," 1994 doctoral thesis, p. 60.

29. Harlene Green, recorded interview with the author, September 26, 2007.

30. Janine Pease-Windy Boy was a long-time member of AIHEC, and a former tribal college president. Her Doctor of Education research was on the development of tribal colleges. She was interviewed in August 2007 for this book because of her association with Patricia Locke, even though she was usually on the other side of highly contentious issues. Much of the material in this section, except where otherwise noted, was based on that interview and her thesis.

31. David M. Gipp, quoted in Janine Pease-Windy Boy, "The Tribally Controlled Community Colleges Act of 1978: An Expansion of Federal Indian Trust Responsibility," 1994 doctoral thesis, p. 63.

32. Gary Kimble, recorded interview with the author.

33. Wayne Stein, recorded interview with the author.

34. Even though they were on opposite sides of most issues, Pease retained a high regard for Patricia. It is not too surprising that these two strong, capable, focused, and determined women would have different views on how to accomplish common objectives. Yet they retained respect for each other and not just as worthy adversaries. Both were mold breakers; both had overcome racism and other obstacles with little encouragement to get their educations; both found criticism and jealousy from among their own people; both were driven by great passion for what they were doing and pushed on toward their objectives with insufficient support and meager resources. On top of it all, they shared the rare and coveted distinction of both being recipients of the MacArthur Fellowship—a most prestigious honor. As one university dean said, "MacArthur is the pinnacle of academic recognition."

35. Tom Aman, "Capital Campaign News," Winter 2006, Sitting Bull College, Ft. Yates, North Dakota, p. 2.

36. "Capital Campaign News," Winter 2006, Sitting Bull College, Ft. Yates, North Dakota, p. 3.

37. Laurel Vermillion: This and all other quotations from Vermillion are from an interview with her on August 21, 2007.

38. David Yarlott: This and all other quotations from Yarlott are from a taped interview with the author on August 23, 2007.

39. Lanny Real Bird: This and all other quotations from Real Bird are from a taped interview with the author on August 23, 2007.

40. Based on an interview with Jerry Henrikson, January 8, 2009. Jerry was a farm boy attending a one-room school near Kathryn, North Dakota. At that time, the author's father traveled to rural schools in North Dakota on behalf of the State Department of Fish and Wildlife to show slides, talk, and recite his original poetry about the wildlife of North Dakota. When the author first met Jerry, he announced, "Your dad changed my life." He explained that after the seeing the slides he asked his parents to buy him all the books they could on wildlife. Instead of staying in farming, as he had intended, he majored in wildlife management in college and took a position with the Bureau of Indian Affairs, which assigned him to a position in Ft. Yates, where he met Patricia and Kevin Locke.

41. Edwin Richardson, based on an interview with the author, August 31, 2008.

42. Harriet Sky, recorded interview with the author, July 20, 2008.

43. E-mail from Senator Inouye's office to the author, November 5, 2009.

44. Cornell University Law School, Supreme Court Collection.

45. Patricia Locke, *Mobridge Tribune,* May 4, 1988, p. 5.

46. Harlene Greene, recorded interview with the author, September 26, 2008.

47. Harlene Greene, this section is based on a recorded interview conducted on September 26, 2008.

48. Gary Kimble, this section is based on an interview with the author, April 9, 2008.

49. Material for this chapter was gleaned from a number of recorded talks Patricia gave, as well as interviews from members of her family.

50. Lynes End of Horn, interview with the author, August 2007.

51. Kevin Locke, interview with the author, February 28, 2008.

52. Dorothy Locke, interview with the author, August 19, 2007.

53. Waniya Locke, interview with the author, August 19, 2007.

54. Kimimila Locke, interview with the author, January 15, 2009.

55. Maymangwa Flying Earth-Miranda, recorded comment made at Patricia Locke's funeral.

56. Based on interviews with his mother and aunt, Imogene and Delores Taken Alive, in August 2007.

57. Robert End of Horn, Sr., recorded interview with the author, August 17, 2007.

58. Based on interviews with the End of Horn boys in August 2007.

59. Earl Medicine, interview with the author, August 13, 2007.

60. Sharon Goodhouse, interview with the author, September 1, 2007.

61. Deborah Tiger, interview with the author, August 16, 2007.

62. Frances Makepeace, interview with the author, August 31, 2007.

63. Sean Makepeace, interview with the author, August 31, 2007.

64. Most of the material for this chapter is based on interviews with Duane Claymore and Kevin Locke, April 4, 2009.

65. Larry Atkinson, interview with the author, August 20, 2007. All references to him are from that interview.

66. Patricia Locke, *Mobridge Tribune,* March 4, 1987, p. 5.

67. Ibid., *Mobridge Tribune,* April 15, 1987, p. 5.

68. Irene Anderson, *Mobridge Tribune,* May 12, 1987, p. 5.

69. John Jay, quoted by Patricia Locke, *Mobridge Tribune,* June 17, 1987, p. 5.

70. Patricia Locke, *Mobridge Tribune,* February 10, 1988, p. 5. The article quotes David Nichols from his book *Lincoln and the Indians: Civil War Policy and Politics* published by Minnesota University Press, 1978. This reference provides a wealth of information on many repressive documents signed by Lincoln, including the ones leading to the expeditions of 1864 and 1865, to kill as many Indians as possible. These were part of the Lincoln administration's official policy to annihilate all Indians who would not assimilate.

71. Ibid.

72. Patricia Locke, *Mobridge Tribune,* July 1, 1988, p. 5.

73. Ibid., *Mobridge Tribune,* January 4, 1989, p. 5.

74. Ibid., *Mobridge Tribune,* September, 1989, p. 5.

75. This book is still available through Amazon.com.

76. Patricia Locke, *Mobridge Tribune,* February 21, 1990, p. 5.

77. Ibid., *Mobridge Tribune,* August 29, 1990, p. 5.

78. Ibid.

79. Ibid., *Mobridge Tribune,* May 9, 1990, p. 5.

80. Ibid.

81. Ibid.

82. House Executive Document No. 1, 50th Congress, 1st session, serial #2542, pp. 21–22, cited by Patricia Locke, *Mobridge Tribune,* November 14, 1990, p. 5.

83. Patricia Locke, *Mobridge Tribune,* November 28, 1990, p. 5.

84. Ibid.

85. Patricia Locke, *Mobridge Tribune,* April 4, 1991, p. 5.

86. The quotations and most of the material for this chapter are based on the three articles Patricia wrote in the *Mobridge Tribune* starting on October 26, 1988, and an interview with Jacqueline Left Hand Bull conducted in Rapid City, South Dakota on July 13, 2007.

87. Kevin learned of the Bahá'í Faith through Jerry Henrikson and enrolled while the Henriksons stayed with them for several days just before they left the Reservation for the Falkland Islands.

88. Jacqueline Left Hand Bull, op. cit 2008. All quotes from her are from that interview.

89. Guy Marco, interview with the author, April 8, 2010.

90. Dorothy Nelson, based on an interview with the author, July 23, 2008.

91. Jacqueline Left Hand Bull, op. cit.

92. During these conversations, Kevin thought of his mother's Indian name, Tȟawáčhiŋ Wašté Wíŋ, and her becoming a Bahá'í. He thought that, in their essence, names should have a spiritual significance as well as being descriptive and useful for identification. He related this to a passage in the Bahá'í writings. In the Arabic Hidden Words, Bahá'u'lláh says: "O SON OF MAN! I loved thy creation, hence I created thee. Wherefore, do thou love Me, that I may name thy name and fill thy soul with the spirit of life." (Bahá'u'lláh, Hidden Words, Arabic, no. 4.) He felt that his mother's Indian name was her true identity and most likely the name Bahá'u'lláh would use to "name thy name."

93. Shoghi Effendi, *Bahá'í Administration,* p. 88.

94. Jack McCants, based on an interview with the author May 15, 2009. All quotes from him are from that interview.

95., Rúhíyyih Khánum Rabbani, *Alaska Bahá'í News,* No. 162, November 1973:5.

96. James Nelson: This and other quotes from him are from an interview, November 4, 2008.

97. Rúhíyyih Khánum, conversation with the author, December 1960.

98. Jacqueline Left Hand Bull, op. cit.

99. Most of this chapter is based on an interview with Kevin, May 27, 2009.

100. Quoted in the National Women's Hall of Fame "Induction Weekend" brochure, October 7–8, 2005, p. 13.

101. Sharon Goodhouse, op. cit.

102, National Women's Hall of Fame "Induction Weekend" brochure, October 7–8, 2005, p. 13.

103. Gary Kimble, interview with the author, April 9, 2008.

104. Bahá'u'lláh, *Gleanings from the Writings of Bahá'u'lláh*, no. 4.2.

105. The Biblical account is found in Genesis 11:2–9; Bahá'u'lláh confirms this story in *Gleanings from the Writings of Bahá'u'lláh*, no. 87.

106. Bahá'u'lláh, *Gleanings from the Writings of Bahá'u'lláh*, no. 117.

107. 'Abdu'l-Bahá, *Some Answered Questions*, p. 18.

108. 'Abdu'l-Bahá, *Tablets of the Divine Plan*, p. 33.

109. 'Abdu'l-Bahá, *Paris Talks*, no. 22.5–6.

110. From a letter written on behalf of Shoghi Effendi to the National Spiritual Assembly of Central America and Mexico, dated August 22, 1957, quoted in *Lights of Guidance*, no. 2029.

111. 'Abdu'l-Bahá, *Tablets of the Divine Plan*, p. 32.

A SELECTED BIBLIOGRAPHY

Works of Bahá'u'lláh

Gleanings from the Writings of Bahá'u'lláh. Translated by Shoghi Effendi. Wilmette, IL: Bahá'í Publishing, 2005.

Works of 'Abdu'l-Bahá

Paris Talks: Addresses Given by 'Abdu'l-Bahá in 1911. Wilmette, IL: Bahá'í Publishing, 2006.
Some Answered Questions. Compiled and translated by Laura Clifford Barney. 1st pocket-size ed. Wilmette, IL: Bahá'í Publishing Trust, 1984.
Tablets of the Divine Plan. 1st pocket-size ed. Wilmette, IL: Bahá'í Publishing Trust, 1993.

Works of Shoghi Effendi

Bahá'í Administration: Selected Messages 1922–1932. 7th ed. Wilmette, IL: Bahá'í Publishing Trust, 1974.

Other Works

Brown, Dee. *Bury My Heart at Wounded Knee.* Holt, Rinehart & Winston: New York, Chicago, San Francisco, 1971.
Churchill, Ward. *Kill the Indian, Save the Man: The Genocidal Impact of American Indian Residential Schools.* City Lights Publishers: San Francisco, 2004.

Dillon, Richard *North American Indian Wars*. Booksales: New York, 1993.

Pease-Windy Boy, Janine. "The Tribally Controlled Community Colleges Act of 1978: An Expansion of Federal Indian Trust Responsibility," 1994 doctoral thesis.

Walker, James R. *Lakota Belief and Ritual*. University of Nebraska Press and Bison Books: Lincoln, NE, 1991.

William K. Powers, *Ogalala Religion*. University of Nebraska Press: Lincoln, NE, 1977.

Additional Resources

In addition to the interviews, following are the primary resources, plus extensive use of the internet, that were used in researching background information for this material:

Bahá'í Archives, Wilmette, Illinois

Locke, Patricia. Audio tape of a talk given at Chautauqua, 1996

Locke, Patricia. Documentary video at her home on the Standing Rock Reservation in 1991

Locke, Patricia. Video tape of a speech given at the University of Southern Maine, early 1990s

Mobridge Tribune archives

Montana State Library

North Dakota State Library

South Dakota State Library

Western Interstate Consortium for Higher Education archives

Index

Bahá'í
PUBLISHING

Bahá'í Publishing and the Bahá'í Faith

Bahá'í Publishing produces books based on the teachings of the Bahá'í Faith. Founded over 160 years ago, the Bahá'í Faith has spread to some 235 nations and territories and is now accepted by more than five million people. The word "Bahá'í" means "follower of Bahá'u'lláh." Bahá'u'lláh, the founder of the Bahá'í Faith, asserted that He is the Messenger of God for all of humanity in this day. The cornerstone of His teachings is the establishment of the spiritual unity of humankind, which will be achieved by personal transformation and the application of clearly identified spiritual principles. Bahá'ís also believe that there is but one religion and that all the Messengers of God—among them Abraham, Zoroaster, Moses, Krishna, Buddha, Jesus, and Muḥammad—have progressively revealed its nature. Together, the world's great religions are expressions of a single, unfolding divine plan. Human beings, not God's Messengers, are the source of religious divisions, prejudices, and hatreds.

The Bahá'í Faith is not a sect or denomination of another religion, nor is it a cult or a social movement. Rather, it is a globally recognized independent world religion founded on new books of scripture revealed by Bahá'u'lláh.

Bahá'í Publishing is an imprint of the National Spiritual Assembly of the Bahá'ís of the United States.

For more information about the Bahá'í Faith,
or to contact Bahá'ís near you,
visit http://www.bahai.us/
or call
1-800-22-UNITE

OTHER BOOKS AVAILABLE FROM
BAHÁ'Í PUBLISHING

REJOICE IN MY GLADNESS
THE LIFE OF ṬÁHIRIH
Janet Ruhe-Schoen
$18.00 U.S. / $20.00 CAN
Trade Paper
ISBN 978-1-931847-84-1

A moving biography of one of the leading feminists of the 1800s, *Rejoice in My Gladness* traces the story of Ṭáhirih, a woman who began teaching the equality between men and women in largely Muslim Persia, and was eventually martyred for her outspokenness and courage.

Drawing on extensive research and steeped in the culture of daily life in nineteenth-century Persia, this is the definitive account of the life of Ṭáhirih—a renowned poetess and one of the leading feminists of her time. *Rejoice in My Gladness* follows the life of Ṭáhirih from her birth through her adulthood, covering important events such as her marriage, her controversial conversion to the Bábí Faith, and her execution due to her beliefs and activities. The reader will see how Ṭáhirih changed the face of women's rights forever, as she was the first woman in recorded Middle Eastern history to remove her veil before an assembly of men. At her execution, her last words have been recorded as "You can kill me as soon as you like, but you will never stop the emancipation of women."

THE QUICKENING
UNKNOWN POETRY OF ṬÁHIRIH
John S. Hatcher and Amrollah Hemmat
$18.00 U.S. / $20.00 CAN
Trade Paper
ISBN 978-1-931847-83-4

A new priceless collection of previously unpublished poems by the renowned nineteenth-century poetess, Ṭáhirih.

The Quickening is a newly translated collection of stirring poems by the renowned nineteenth-century poetess Ṭáhirih that deal with a subject that has challenged religious scholars throughout the ages. Among the world religions, no theme has attracted more attention or caused more controversy than the concept of a last judgment or end of time. The Bahá'í view of the "Resurrection," or the "Quickening," as the term is translated here, stands in bold contrast to many traditional views. It is seen as a prelude to a glorious outcome—the galvanizing of our collective will to bring about a just and lasting peace and the unification of humankind. In addition to the beautifully crafted English translation of Ṭáhirih's poems, this volume also includes her work in the original Persian and Arabic.

SPIRIT OF FAITH
THE ONENESS OF RELIGION
Bahá'í Publishing
$12.00 U.S. / $14.00 CAN
Hardcover
ISBN 978-1-931847-81-0

Spirit of Faith: The Oneness of Religion is a compilation of writings and prayers that focus on the inherent oneness of all the world's great religions. Spiritual seekers of all faiths will relish these uplifting passages that underscore the unity of thought that helps us define our place within a single, unfolding, and divine creation. This collection contains writings from Bahá'u'lláh, the Báb, and 'Abdu'l-Bahá.

The *Spirit of Faith* series will explore a range of topics—such as the unity of humanity, the eternal covenant of God, the promise of world peace, and much more—by taking an in-depth look at how the writings of the Bahá'í Faith view these issues. The series is designed to encourage readers of all faiths to think about spirituality, and to take time to pray and meditate on these important topics.

TALKS BY 'ABDU'L-BAHÁ
THE ETERNAL COVENANT
'Abdu'l-Bahá
$14.00 U.S. / $16.00 CAN
Hardcover
ISBN 978-1-931847-82-7

Spiritually uplifting and thought-provoking collection of talks from one of the central figures of the Bahá'í Faith.

Talks by 'Abdu'l-Bahá is a collection of talks given by 'Abdu'l-Bahá—the son and appointed successor of Bahá'u'lláh, the Prophet and Founder of the Bahá'í Faith—during his historic journey to North America in 1912. Speaking in front of diverse audiences, 'Abdu'l-Bahá offered profound insights on a number of topics in a simple manner accessible to anyone who listened with an open heart. The talks included in this volume all relate to the theme of the eternal covenant of God, one of the central themes of the teachings of the Bahá'í Faith. According to this covenant, God never leaves humankind alone without guidance but rather makes His will and purpose known to us through the appearance of His Prophets or Manifestations, Who appear periodically throughout history in order to advance human civilization.